THE CONFLICT

THE SEPARATION OF CHURCH AND STATE

CLAYTON L. NUTTALL

REGULAR BAPTIST PRESS
1300 North Meacham Road
Post Office Box 95500
Schaumburg, Illinois 60195

Library of Congress Cataloging in Publication Data

Nuttall, Clayton L.
The conflict—the separation of church and state.

I. Church and state in the United States.
I. Title.
BR516.N8 322'.1'0973 80-21267
ISBN 0-87727-076-9

THE CONFLICT—THE SEPARATION OF CHURCH AND STATE

Regular Baptist Press
Schaumburg, Illinois
Printed in U.S.A.

To my wife, Ruth, who has remained a strong pillar in our home and ministry.

I express my deep gratitude to Darlene Ryan for endless hours of preparing and revising the typed manuscript; to Shirley Landstrom and Judy Price for detail work; and to the Reverend John Wood, Attorney Mike Thomas, Dr. David Gibbs, Attorney Mike Craze and Dr. Paul Tassell for reading the manuscript and their guidance in revision.

Contents

Introduction

It is my opinion that Clay Nuttall has rendered the churches of America an invaluable service by writing this book. In my ministry of working with Baptist churches in the state of Michigan, I saw sometime ago that church and state were on a collision course, and that time has now arrived. Pastor Nuttall does not write about war from the perspective of a freshly graduated West Point cadet. He writes as a soldier who has been in the trenches and knows the smell of gunpowder. He has been there and knows the trauma of a court battle. He has also experienced the sweet odor of victory. I heartily recommend this book to any and all who value their religious freedoms. "They are coming up the stairs, and they have chains in their hands."

— John R. Wood, State Representative
Michigan Association of Regular Baptist Churches

Preface

Conflict is nothing new for committed Christians. Volumes have been written which detail the suffering of those who chose to stand on their convictions. This book is a warning to all dedicated believers. The Biblical church is in danger in the United States. While we should not play the role of alarmist, we must sound a clear note on the trumpet. We are approaching persecution from the state. Every balanced church ministry should review its position, standard and direction.

This material is not presented from the viewpoint of a scholar but a thinker. Sharing cold, static information and listing statistics is not within the purpose of this work. It is committed to motivate leadership to cautious action. In the work, *The Christian Mind,* by Harry Blamires, there is an explanation of the definition of the thinker's viewpoint.

> The scholar evades decisiveness; he hesitates to praise or condemn; he balances conclusion against competing conclusion so as to cancel out conclusiveness; he is tentative, skeptical, uncommitted. The thinker hates indecision and confusion; he firmly distinguishes right from wrong, good from evil; he is at home in a world of clearly demarcated categories and proven conclusions; he is dogmatic and committed; he works towards decisive action.
>
> To typify the extremes in this way is useful, but must not be taken too literally. For the scholar, as thus characterized, is not the only man who studies: and the thinker, as thus characterized, is not the only man who thinks. Obviously there is no scholar who does not think; and there is no thinker who is quite devoid of scholarship.[1]

One should never make an apology for being scholarly, but life is too brief to write without moving purpose.

The historical and legal material recorded herein is only meant to be a brief summary to set the stage. These are needed only to clarify our present plight. It is incredible that we could have known so little or have forgotten so much about the suffering of those whose pain paved the way for our religious freedom. Too many speak too lightly about such things as the taxation of churches and licensing of her ministries. For this reason the discussion of the Biblical record of the separation of church and state is meant to be thorough. The authority of the Word of God is still the final test of the dissenter's felicity.

The current conflict is based on a little recognized fact. The state is determined to separate the church from the state, but is equally determined to increase the attachment of the state to the church. Believers must maintain the historical principle of the separation of the church and the state.

Footnote

1. Harry Blamires, *The Christian Mind* (Ann Arbor: Servant Books, 1963), p. 51.

ONE

Introduction to Conflict

". . . More than all, a government and a country were to commence, with the very first foundations laid under the divine light of the Christian religions. . . . Who would wish that his country's existence had otherwise begun? Let us not forget the religious character of our origin" (Daniel Webster).

The Cycle

THAT HISTORY REPEATS itself is demonstrated consistently in the annals of time. As we read past narratives we feel that they are records of the present. One excellent illustration of this is the book of Judges. Israel repeatedly moved through the cycle of power, disobedience, bondage, repentance and deliverance. The Old Testament is filled with such examples.

Those who hold a dispensational view of Scripture would recognize this. God establishes a plan for man—*oikonomia,* law of the house, or economy. He demonstrates through this His sovereignty by providing an environment and government. Each dispensation ends with crisis, a confession of man's fallibility. The order is establishment, disobedience and crisis.

This point of view is further illustrated in the rise and fall of world empires and the continuing power struggle in the old world. It is also clearly stated in the record of Western Christianity.

> This cycle is a familiar phase of the history of western Christianity. The quakers arose in protest against the inadequacies of institutionalized Christianity in seventeenth-century England and brought to their interpretation of the teachings of Jesus a naive and uncritical realism which made them dangerous radicals. They were bitterly persecuted both in England and New England. During the last half of the seventeenth and the first quarter of the eighteenth century, they fought a great battle for religious liberty against the intolerant New England theocracies.[1]

The American Christian community has passed through the cycle of freedom, persecution and dissent. Conflict was not left behind in the land of the Reformation or England. In some cases the persecuted became the persecutors in the new land. Their intolerance was often carried out with as much violence as that which they had suffered.

Our nation has always known the presence of the dissenter, separatist and nonconformist. It is a way of life and the American privilege. Dissenters from the Christian community have suffered greatly on this soil we call "the land of the free and the home of the brave." The question to consider in this cyclical move is this, "When might we expect a recurrence of persecution?"

The Conflict

While conflict is never dead, it smolders. That which our forefathers had won by blood and death was established and recorded in constitutional law. We were free to practice our convictions but not to harass those with other convictions. The state was forbidden to prohibit the free exercise of religion and, at the same time, the government could no longer establish a "licit" religion. In isolated areas these laws were violated by powerful religious groups and localized governments, but as a whole they were effective.

Let no one assume that because religious freedom is on the books of law we can expect it to be perpetually recognized. We need only remember that all the Iron Curtain countries have some form of law declaring religious freedom. It is not a question of existence; it is a question of recognition and practice.

The passing years brought an apathy on the part of the church. The separation of powers, described in our foundational legal document, has become unbalanced. This can be seen in what has been referred to as the "superstructure of our nation." We were born and formed in the framework of Christian principles. Our basic laws had their roots in the standards of God's holy Word. Some currently claim that our foundation was humanism. That is a prefabrication of the most terrible order. One need only listen to the words of our founders and national leaders:

> SAMUEL ADAMS: The rights of the Colonists as Christians . . . may be best understood by reading and carefully studying the institution of the great Law Giver and Head of the Christian Church, which are to be found clearly written and promulgated in the New Testament.[2]

> DANIEL WEBSTER: . . . More than all, a government and a country were to commence, with the very first foundations laid under the divine light of the Christian religion. . . . Who would wish that his country's existence had otherwise begun? Let us not forget the religious character of our origin.[3]

> JOHN QUINCY ADAMS: From the day of the Declaration . . . They [the American people] were bound by the laws of God, which they all, and by the laws of the Gospel, which they nearly all, acknowledged as the rules of their conduct.[4]

> ABRAHAM LINCOLN: Unless the great God who assisted him [Washington] shall be with me and aid me, I must fail; but if the same omniscient mind and mighty arm that directed and protected him shall guide and support me, I shall not fail—I shall succeed. Let us all pray that the God of our fathers may not forsake us now.[5]

To be assured, our moorings were Christian: "America—the only nation in history ever to establish a government and a Constitution upon principles of Christian liberty derived from the Word of God—America forgot."[6]

American Education

An excellent illustration of this is the American educational system. Schools in this land were conducted by the church, in the church and through the church leadership. Community education was a follower. One can only ponder the motives of the church in allowing education to become public rather than Christian. The rationale may well have been that both could be accomplished; that is, the education of the church and the general populace at the same time. In any case, a marriage was arranged. More pointedly, the church served as a common law wife of this union. We can lay at the feet of Horace Mann and the corrupt progressivism of Dewey the ultimate putrification of this strange collusion.

> In the years 1837-1848 Horace Mann, whom John Dewey designated as the *"father of progressive education,"* made a series of Annual Reports to the Massachusetts Board of Education of which he was Secretary. These Reports paved the way for a state financed, state directed, and ultimately a state controlled education program superseding local control through the demand for "standardization" of school structures, textbooks, curriculum, and teacher training and certification. But even this might not have proved so effective in the "secularization" of education had we not deliberately removed the Bible as the basis of our Christian character and substituted for salvation and regeneration of heart a *psychological atheism* which found man innately "good" and society "bad."[7]

In any case, it remained thus until the early 1950s: a public religious education. By then the power of public education was in the community and increasingly under the power of the state and federal bureaucracy. The children of the church were caught in the trap and it closed.

The 1950s and 1960s saw the purging of religion from the schools. A large number of people were concerned and protested. Several legislative acts were introduced to correct this. A small amount of this activism continued late into the 1970s. Many Christians felt that it was not within the constitutional direction for the government to establish religion in the government schools. Some of them still do not realize that this problem came because the church gave up her schools to the state.

> But the subversion of Christianity through education did not occur easily in a nation so dedicated to fulfilling God's purpose for America. And while we might be tempted to believe that the accomplishment of this secularization of education occurred when the highest court in our land—the Supreme Court—ruled on the Prayer Case of 1962, it is not so. One cannot legislate Christianity out of a nation through the courts—it must occur first through *individual acceptance* of an educational system without God or Christ as its foundation. Thus, the records show, that when individuals, churches, communities

> yielded up to the state the control and direction of education it was then that the Bible became *"as the words of a book that is sealed."*[8]

The ban of prayer and the Bible from the government schools was only a part of the overall struggle. A pagan religious view known as humanism triumphed in textbook and teacher. It is not so much a question of prayer and Bible in the school, but was the church right in making an unequal yoke with the state in education? What seemed to be easy or right has now become a national tragedy. We discovered that within the framework of the existing education it was impossible for the church to fulfill the portion of the Great Commission that requires the education of the church. Distinctly, this is to evangelize, enlist and educate (Matt. 28:19, 20).

What had been church education had become public schools, and these had become government schools in the 1950s, followed by the trauma of the 1970s when they became state schools. The state then held an educational monopoly, not only on the funds of the state, but also the funds of the church. That money was taken in the form of educational taxes and the state refused to return it. When the church said, "We will train our children in the church," the state replied, "We might let you do that, but you will have to pay twice." To add insult to injury, the state demanded the authority to regulate any system that rose to challenge it, mainly private education.

This challenge came at an ironic time. The *state school* had failed in its overall approach. Large schools and those in the inner city were characterized by violence, rape, vandalism and mayhem. The system as a whole failed to provide basic education. Students who were barely able to read were graduated from secondary schools. Grade inflation swept the establishment in an effort to provide credibility. God had been expelled from the classroom along with morality and reality. It was this pitiful, ragged, emaciated character that the powerful bureaucracy demanded the church use as a standard.

The final chapter in this illustration of American education was written in the last days of the 1970s. Education that had passed from the church to community, to the public and then to government and state began its final move to federal education. Under the administration of President Jimmy Carter, a cabinet level authority (a federal Department of Education) was imposed upon the people. An elementary understanding of the foregoing transition leaves only one intelligent conclusion: Local school organizations have lost any sensible level of community control.

Such a statement is not an exaggeration or prophecy. We were warned as early as 1972 as stated in *The National Laymen's Digest* article entitled, "Federal Grip on Schools Tightens."

> The Youth Development Bureau within the Department of Health, Education and Welfare has published "THE RIGHTS AND RESPONSIBILITIES OF STUDENTS: A HANDBOOK FOR THE SCHOOL COMMUNITY" available from the Director, Office for Civil Rights of Region V, 300 South Wacker Drive, Chicago, Illinois 60606, one of the 10 regions established in the United States by Executive Order of Richard Nixon in 1972.
>
> On page vi of the booklet, Larry L. Dye, Director of the Youth Development Bureau, says, among other things:
>
> > "The Youth Development Bureau takes the position that young people have the right to participate in the institutions that affect their lives."
>
> There follows, in the rest of the booklet, two important divisions: first "The Federal Framework", and then "A model code for the school community." There is much informative material and some good sound advice for parents, teachers, and school board members—no quarrel on that! The alarming thing is that we have a federal youth DEVELOPMENT bureau. More frightening is the stated fact that a DIRECTOR, in fact *THE* director of that bureau, has "TAKEN A POSITION" that affects all the schools of the nation and in one fell sweep deprives parents of their God-given rights at the same time that it curtails and effectually controls the decisions a board of education can make and enforce. Indeed, Big Brother has come to watch over the whole process, ordering all in accord with the "position it has taken". Sometimes that position is benign, but, in many cases, it has been the cause of what we deplore in the whole process of public education: more money for less learning with a precipitous decline in morality.[9]

More shocking than all of this is what this means to the church schools. No valid educational ministry of a Biblical New Testament church could begin to implement the anti-Biblical guidelines, the humanistic philosophy that permeates these writings. This is further demonstrated.

> As one peruses the contents of this booklet, he can see how certain "positions taken" account for dire consequences when translated into actions and restraints mandated by federal law

and interpreted by the courts. One of the most important "rights" of students under the "Federal Framework", p. 3, is the following:

> "Students have the right to observe any religion (or none at all, if they wish). The school shall not interfere with the right by requiring, establishing, or conducting religious exercises, nor by implementing policies that favor one religion over another or religion over non-religion."[10]

What we had feared has become a reality: a computer mentality at the national level, free to oppress the church with only one reply to the ministries it is destroying, "We are only doing our job." Those who despise God and His authority were ready for the institution of federal schools.

The church, in the meantime, had used the greatest tool of education, the Bible, to produce a miracle. With its money for education forcibly removed by the state, with a young staff and a minority of buildings, the church produced a crop of graduates that outstripped the poor fruit of secular humanism. The state not only failed to be embarrassed, it was bold enough to say that the church must operate by their standards or go to court.

> We have seen that the Ohio Department of Education views the interpretative sections as legally binding on Christian schools, and that the Ohio Supreme Court, while touching on this issue, did not decide it. The threat of legal coercion is therefore possible, but that is always the case when churches allow their ministries to be controlled by the state.[11]

The battle lines were clearly drawn. The freedom to educate the children of the church had been abrogated. To regain the precious privilege, one of two things would have to transpire. The state would need to lay aside its claims or conflict would ensue. The conflict came, first in little, out-of-the-way places and then on a national scale.

One well-known case was the right of the Amish people to practice their convictions and educate their own children. They won. Then a simple pastor, Levi Whisner, challenged the powerful bureaucracy in Ohio with a landmark struggle that seemed to stir the dynamic churches of America to action. Many others followed and emerged victorious from the conflict. Much of the activity of the 1970s was in the courtroom. As the era closed, however, a dark cloud has begun to cover the church. Some, like Lester Roloff, have found conflict has carried them to jail and prison, and some have suffered the loss of earthly possessions.

Christian Apathy

The saddest thing of all is the rampant apathy among Christians. A few saw the handwriting on the wall in the 1950s, others only recently, and many are still asleep. To them the suffering church, in the coming conflict, will cry as Paul cried to the Roman Christians.

> And that, knowing the time, that now it is high time to awake out of sleep: for now is our salvation nearer than when we believed.
>
> The night is far spent, the day is at hand: let us therefore cast off the works of darkness, and let us put on the armour of light.
>
> Let us walk honestly, as in the day; not in rioting and drunkenness, not in [immorality] and wantonness, not in strife and envying.
>
> But put ye on the Lord Jesus Christ, and make not provision for the flesh, to fulfil the lusts thereof (Rom. 13:11-14).

A brief overview of our subject leaves one consideration. There is no alternative. Persecution will come to the church in America as a result of the conflict in which we are now engaged. The greatest sadness, however, will not come to those who now suffer nor to those who will be incarcerated. Grief will come to those true children of God who did not know, or would not know and when they did know refused to stand with their brothers. From a lofty perch they extolled Caesar and praised their own reticence to stoop to controversy. Only the *bema* will reveal the anguish of leaders who castigated fellow pastors when they were crushed under the heel of the sovereign state.

I remember hearing as a young child the stories that came from postwar Germany. Many godly pastors and church leaders were executed because they would not obey Nazi dictates to the church. The conformers who led their churches to Hitler as blind leaders of the blind found, too late for most of them, that they had only postponed their death. For those who survived: How could they face their people? It would have been better to "obey God rather than men" and accept the conflict.

How far will this hour of trouble carry us? It is more than possible that the closing of this century will see the church in a trial of persecution worse than any we have ever known in this land. How did it happen? Where are we now? Is it too late?

Footnotes

1. John M. Mecklin, *The Story of American Dissent* (New York: Harcourt, Brace and Co., 1934), p. 4.

2. Report of the Committee of Correspondence to the Boston Town Meeting, November 20, 1772.

3. Bicentennial speech at Plymouth, Massachusetts, celebrating the landing of the Pilgrims, 1820.

4. An address delivered July 4, 1821, from the rostrum of the House of Representatives on the occasion of reading the Declaration of Independence.

5. Farewell address in Springfield, Illinois, on February 11, 1861, before taking office of President of the United States.

6. Rosalie J. Slater, *Teaching and Learning America's Christian History* (San Francisco: Foundation for American Christian Education, 1973), p. 52.

7. Ibid., pp. 52, 53.

8. Ibid., p. 52.

9. "Federal Grip on Schools Tightens," *The National Laymen's Digest* (November 1979), pp. 1, 2.

10. Ibid., p. 2.

11. Alan N. Grover, *Ohio's Trojan Horse* (Greenville, SC: Bob Jones University Press, 1977), p. 85.

TWO

The Biblical Issue

"For rulers are not a terror to good works, but to the evil. Wilt thou then not be afraid of the power? do that which is good, and thou shalt have praise of the same" (Rom. 13:3).

IT IS PARAMOUNT that we recognize the separation of church and state as a Biblical issue. In the confines of temporal law, the standard is constantly changing. With the Word of God it is static and timeless. The highest authority in this conflict, therefore, is the Word of God.

Romans 13 appears to be the central New Testament passage in this area. "Nothing in the entire Bible is more important to the subject of the place of human civil government in the providence of God than is this text."[1] Let us dissect the message carefully.

> Let every soul be subject unto the higher powers. For there is no power but of God: the powers that be are ordained of God.
>
> Whosoever therefore resisteth the power, resisteth the ordinance of God: and they that resist shall receive to themselves damnation.
>
> For rulers are not a terror to good works, but to the evil. Wilt thou then not be afraid of the power? do that which is good, and thou shalt have praise of the same:
>
> For he is the minister of God to thee for good. But if thou do that which is evil, be afraid; for he beareth not the sword in vain:

> for he is the minister of God, a revenger to execute wrath upon him that doeth evil.
>
> Wherefore ye must needs be subject, not only for wrath, but also for conscience sake.
>
> For this cause pay ye tribute also: for they are God's ministers, attending continually upon this very thing.
>
> Render therefore to all their dues: tribute to whom tribute is due; custom to whom custom; fear to whom fear; honour to whom honour (Rom. 13:1-7).

What we discover is a summary teaching of the total doctrine.

1. God has ordained all powers, and the world has three major areas of authority: (a) the home with the father as the earthly head (Eph. 5:22-24; 6:1-4); (b) the church with the pastor as the earthly head (Heb. 13:7, 17); (c) the state with the king as the earthly head (1 Pet. 2:13, 14).

2. Everyone is subject to those powers, but they are all answerable to God. The husband-father is subject to Christ (1 Cor. 11:3). The pastor-teacher is subject to the Chief Shepherd (Heb. 13:17, 20; 1 Pet. 5:1-4). The king is limited to God's granted power (John 19:11) and is, therefore, a minister of God.

3. Specific responsibilities are given to each power and balanced with the understanding that they are not to infringe upon each other. These powers are equal and sovereign in their assigned areas.

The State

Among the responsibilities assigned to the state is the exacting of tribute. Taxes are received to assist the government in the waging of war for the protection of the people. This is demonstrated in the Old Testament where the nation was commanded to fight for the defense of its citizens. The government is also charged with the responsibility of punishing evildoers. "He" (meaning the government) is the "minister of God" in enforcing God's laws in the nation. It is not the prerogative of the state to arbitrarily make laws that are in contrast to God's clear commands.

Only the state has the power to take life, as directed by God. "For he is the minister of God to thee for good. But if thou do that which is evil, be afraid; for he beareth not the sword in vain: for he is the minister of God, a revenger to execute wrath upon him that doeth evil" (Rom. 13:4).

It is clear that the state is limited in its provision for the common citizenship, its punishment of evildoers and defensive protection of the general populace. That limitation is described as ordained of God and answerable to God . . . terror to evil and not to good works . . . wrath to the disobedient and not to the obedient. But the clear precept is that the state is carrying out God's mandate and only then will the righteous "have praise of the same" (v. 3). "When the righteous are in authority, the people rejoice: but when the wicked beareth rule, the people mourn" (Prov. 29:2).

The Church

While the ministry of the church is not spelled out in this passage, it is identified as the "good works . . . [those] subject . . . for conscience sake" (Rom. 13:3, 5). The responsibility of the church is clarified in the Great Commission (Matt. 28:18-20). It is namely to evangelize, enlist and educate. These are, in fact, the areas that God has granted to the church. The state is restrained from hindering this total ministry. It is also required to protect the righteous outworking of the church. We do not speak of providing for the work of the church or carrying it out. The government by noninterference protects the church from oppression and persecution which is its legitimate responsibility. In this area it is interesting to note that nowhere does the Bible give the responsibility of education to the state.

It is also imperative that we recognize that the state does not grant freedom to the church. This has been granted by God, and the state only recognizes what God has set in order. The same is true, as we shall discuss later, in the matter of taxation. The state does not grant tax exemption for the church, it only recognizes what God has provided. Since it does not give freedom or a tax-free status, it is not empowered to remove or withhold it.

The Home

We view this basic care by the state for the church and home as the protection of "good works." The home's responsibilities are summarized for us in Titus 2. Many other passages speak to discipline and training, but the limitation of home authority is best described in its responsibility. It is important to note that the home is limited to its single structure. When homes begin to function collectively, they fall under the authority of one of the above.

Romans presents for us limitation to authority; namely, that civil powers are responsible to God to carry out *His will*. They speak with power only in those areas assigned and only when they carry out His direction. Since this is true, we are faced with a serious question. Why are we commanded, "Submit yourselves to every ordinance of man . . ." (1 Pet. 2:13)?

The key words in this passage in 1 Peter build a strong bridge from the previous Romans discussion. These are *conscience, good works, the Lord's sake* and *the will of God*. It is clearly understood that human government is predicated on the principle that it carries out God's will to protect and bless those who obey God. It would be wise to look at the whole passage.

> Dearly beloved, I beseech you as strangers and pilgrims, abstain from fleshly lusts, which war against the soul;
>
> Having your conversation honest among the Gentiles: that, whereas they speak against you as evildoers, they may by your good works, which they shall behold, glorify God in the day of visitation.
>
> Submit yourselves to every ordinance of man for the Lord's sake: whether it be to the king, as supreme;
>
> Or unto governors, as unto them that are sent by him for the punishment of evildoers, and for the praise of them that do well.
>
> For so is the will of God, that with well doing ye may put to silence the ignorance of foolish men:
>
> As free, and not using your liberty for a cloak of maliciousness, but as the servants of God.
>
> Honour all men. Love the brotherhood. Fear God. Honour the king (1 Pet. 2:11-17).

Carefully note that the ordinances of man that are to be obeyed are specifically the commands of God. They are not obeyed because man wrote them, but because God wrote them. The context of this passage makes the purpose of government gloriously clear. Our submission to the state, in its legitimate areas, leaves a strong testimony with the government. The purpose, then, is to encourage government to protect us and, therefore, glorify God by making it possible for the work of the church to prosper.

At this point we must ask a second question: What do Christians do when the state makes a law that is against God?

We are given a multitude of warnings in the Word about those who are anarchist in spirit. "My son, fear thou the LORD and the king: and meddle not with them that are given to change" (Prov. 24:21). "But chiefly them that walk after the flesh in the lust of uncleanness, and despise government. Presumptuous are they, selfwilled, they are not afraid to speak evil of dignities. Whereas angels, which are greater in power and might, bring not railing accusation against them before the Lord" (2 Pet. 2:10, 11).

This is where we must use great care. "As free, and not using your liberty for a cloak of maliciousness, but as the servants of God" (1 Pet. 2:16). If we obey God there are times when godly people must disobey the government. The Biblical record demonstrates this. We must remember that in these cases the people of God were not lawbreakers, but they obeyed a higher law. In fact, it was the disobedient state that was lawless in making a law that is not a law and most certainly opposed to God.

> In the New Testament the most outstanding passage bearing on political theory is found in the thirteenth chapter of the epistle to the Romans. Paul here teaches, "Every soul must be in subjection to the higher authorities. There is indeed no authority except under God, and those that exist are ordered under God; so that he who sets himself against the authority has resisted God's arrangement; and those who have resisted will receive for themselves condemnation" (vv. 1 and 2).
>
> We must remember here the principle that we do not have the teaching of the Scripture on any subject unless we have examined all the relevant passages. Not all the qualifications of a complex subject are to be found in any one passage. The principle that one must obey the existing government, and that it is God's will that government shall exist, and that a lawless person is resisting what God has ordained, is perfectly obvious *ceteris paribus.* What Paul is talking about is the kind of government which fulfills the functions described in the context of the immediately following verses. He is not speaking of *de facto* government which is lawless in itself, breaking the laws of God and trampling upon the rights of man.[2]

Lawbreakers?

The story of Moses, the lawgiver, presents us with an excellent example of this. Pharaoh had commanded, by law, that all the male children be killed when they were born (Exod. 1:16). "But the midwives feared God, and did not as the king of Egypt commanded them, but saved the men children alive" (Exod. 1:17). They stood alone and God evidently honored them for it (Exod. 1:21). The parents of Moses were under the law to kill the boy child. They refused.

"By faith Moses, when he was born, was hid three months of his parents, because they saw he was a proper child; and they were not afraid of the king's commandment" (Heb. 11:23). This text says they were not afraid of the king's law. The reason for this was they were obeying a higher law. This very same phrase is used in Romans 13:3, "Wilt thou then not be afraid of the power?" It is the responsibility of the government to praise those who do well (1 Pet. 2:14); but when it praises evil and brings terror to good, we find our peace and lack of fear in obeying God. Moses later expressed this same confidence in obeying God, not the king. "By faith he forsook Egypt, not fearing the wrath of the king: for he endured, as seeing him who is invisible" (Heb. 11:27).

The book of Daniel provides us with two more excellent illustrations. The three Hebrew children were faced with disobeying a temporal power that was not speaking for God. They said:

> . . . O Nebuchadnezzar, we are not careful to answer thee in this matter.
>
> If it be so, our God whom we serve is able to deliver us from the burning fiery furnace, and he will deliver us out of thine hand, O king.
>
> But if not, be it known unto thee, O king, that we will not serve thy gods, nor worship the golden image which thou hast set up (Dan. 3:16-18).

The exciting thing about their obedience to the higher power is the statement of the king himself: "Then Nebuchadnezzar spake, and said, Blessed be the God of Shadrach, Meshach, and Abed-nego, who hath sent his angel, and delivered his servants that trusted in him, and have changed the king's word, and yielded their bodies, that they might not serve nor worship any god, except their own God" (Dan. 3:28).

Daniel was also faced with a law that would cause him to violate God, but he obeyed God. "Now when Daniel knew that the writing was signed, he went into his house; and his windows being open in his chamber toward Jerusalem, he kneeled upon his knees three times a day, and prayed, and gave thanks before his God, as he did aforetime. Then these men assembled, and found Daniel praying and making supplication before his God" (Dan. 6:10, 11).

From the lions' den Daniel proclaimed his righteous loyalty to the king and God: "My God hath sent his angel, and hath shut the lions' mouths, that they have not hurt me: forasmuch as before him innocency was found in me; and also before thee, O king, have I done no hurt" (Dan. 6:22). In fact, he was more faithful to the king than those who obeyed him. Daniel was a true patriot.

The Acts of the Apostles records an enormous number of incidents where in obeying God a righteous man seemingly disobeyed the state.

> And Annas the high priest, and Caiaphas, and John, and Alexander, and as many as were of the kindred of the high priest, were gathered together at Jerusalem.
>
> And they called them, and commanded them not to speak at all nor teach in the name of Jesus.
>
> But Peter and John answered and said unto them, Whether it be right in the sight of God to hearken unto you more than unto God, judge ye.
>
> For we cannot but speak the things which we have seen and heard.
>
> So when they had further threatened them, they let them go, finding nothing how they might punish them, because of the people: for all men glorified God for that which was done.
>
> And now, Lord, behold their threatenings: and grant unto thy servants, that with all boldness they may speak thy word,
>
> By stretching forth thine hand to heal; and that signs and wonders may be done by the name of thy holy child Jesus.
>
> And when they had prayed, the place was shaken where they were assembled together; and they were all filled with the Holy Ghost, and they spake the word of God with boldness.
>
> Saying, Did not we straitly command you that ye should not teach in this name? and, behold, ye have filled Jerusalem with your doctrine, and intend to bring this man's blood upon us.
>
> Then Peter and the other apostles answered and said, We ought to obey God rather than men (Acts 4:6, 18-21, 29-31; 5:28, 29).

Stephen's death, as the first martyr of the church, was a direct result of obeying a higher power. The great persecution of Acts 8 came as a result of the disciples disobeying the temporal authorities and, even then, ". . . they that were scattered abroad went every where preaching the word" (Acts 8:4). This was followed by the death of James (Acts 12:2), whom many feel was the senior pastor of the church of Jerusalem, as well as the imprisonment of Peter (Acts 12:3). What more shall we say, then, of Paul and Silas (Acts 16:23) in a Philippian jail for obeying God, and Paul's imprisonment unto death? The final issue rests in the fact that both writers, Paul and

Peter, who gave us these clear statements on obedience to the state, were men who went to prison for obeying God and what appeared to men as a violation of temporal law. Were these men above the law? No, they obeyed a higher law.

Worship of the State

Materialism is prominent in our day; it is the worship of things. Possessions have become a god. Humanism is the worship of man; it is the religion of the state school. Intellectualism is the worship of the mind; it deifies the intellect. We are cursed this day with a new cult. It is statism—the worship of the state or temporal government. This monster has been made higher than the sovereign God. Can any Biblicist conceive of a supreme court outlawing capital punishment and approving abortion? We live in an hour when pornography is permitted and the church is being crushed. We must obey God Who said, "Thou shalt have no other gods before me" (Exod. 20:3).

The principle of separation is illustrated in 2 Corinthians 6:14-18 and throughout the Old Testament where Israel was to be separate from the Gentile nations (Hos. 11:1; Isa. 7:1-16; Amos 7:1-13). The reason this is so important is because God will not take second place to earthly government. Christ, in fact, is the Head of the Church which is His Body (Col. 1:17, 18). We, therefore, are forbidden to accept any other headship. We may not allow any temporal authority to stand in Christ's stead to certify, license, approve or accredit. We are to fear God (Matt. 10:28), and then we will not fear the state regardless of what it does.

Intrusions

An example of the tragedy of illicit intrusions by the state is found in 2 Chronicles 26:17 and 18.

> And Azariah the priest went in after him, and with him fourscore priests of the LORD, that were valiant men:
>
> And they withstood Uzziah the king, and said unto him, It appertaineth not unto thee, Uzziah, to burn incense unto the LORD, but to the priests the sons of Aaron, that are consecrated to burn incense: go out of the sanctuary; for thou hast trespassed; neither shall it be for thine honour from the LORD God.

Here is a king who is punished by God because he trespassed on religious ground. It is interesting that even Artaxerxes the king decreed in Ezra 7:24, "Also we certify you, that touching any of the priests and Levites, singers, porters, Nethinims, or ministers of this house of God, it shall not be lawful to impose toll, tribute, or custom, upon them." Zerubbabel informed the illicit adversaries, ". . . Ye have nothing to do with us to build an house unto our God . . ." (Ezra 4:3). The truth is that many who claim to obey God's Word as their final rule in faith and practice have really become disobedient. Slowly and quietly we have allowed the state to take the place of Jesus Christ as Head of our churches. That may be the reason why it is so easy for other illicit powers to control and destroy the local church. In many areas we have strayed so far from Bible authority that there is no conscience about giving in to protect our tranquility and affluency.

The Bible demands a wall of separation between the state and church. We are thankful for temporal statutes that agree with God, but they are not the source of authority. God's Word is! It is our desire to have peace. "Paul, an apostle of Jesus Christ by the will of God, according to the promise of life which is in Christ Jesus. To Timothy, my dearly beloved son: Grace, mercy, and peace, from God the Father and Christ Jesus our Lord" (2 Tim. 1:1, 2).

But peace with God does not always mean peace with men or human government, and "We ought to obey God rather than men" (Acts 5:29). In our obeying God in the present conflict, let us be determined that we will "honour all men. Love the brotherhood. Fear God. Honour the king" (1 Pet. 2:17).

Footnotes

1. Robert Duncan Culver, *Toward a Biblical View of Civil Government* (Chicago: Moody Press, 1975), p. 244. Used by permission.

2. James Oliver Buswell, Jr., *A Systematic Theology of the Christian Religion,* Vol. I, *Theism and Biblical Anthropology* (Grand Rapids: Zondervan Publishing House, 1962), p. 402.

THREE

From Pentecost to the Puritans

"Except I can be convinced by clear and conclusive reasoning, or by proofs taken from the Holy Scriptures, I neither can nor will recant, because it is neither safe nor advisable to do anything which is against my conscience. Here I stand. I cannot do otherwise, so help me God! Amen" (Martin Luther).

A VACUUM CANNOT EXIST relative to the power struggle between church and state. There is always a movement to overpower the opposite. What should be desirable for both is a balance. Throughout church history the pendulum has swung to the extreme limits for both. At this present hour the apathy of the church has led to the state becoming a strong overlord.

A Baptist Principle

Baptists have always been marked by a strong view of the separation principle. Not only have our forefathers maintained obedience to the state in matters assigned to them, but just as important, they have maintained a freedom of conscience for other religious views that are not the same as their own. These and other principles are stated in Edward T. Hiscox's guide to the conduct and operation of Baptist churches.

> The Bible is a Divine Revelation given of God to men, and is a complete and infallible guide and standard of authority in all matters of religion and morals; whatever it teaches is to be believed, and whatever it commands is to be obeyed; whatever it commends is to be accepted as both right and useful; whatever it condemns is to be avoided as both wrong and hurtful; but what it neither commands nor teaches is not to be imposed on the conscience as of religious obligation.[1]

That the Word of God is used for such authority in the common relationships of man is further clarified by Hiscox.

> The New Testament is the constitution of Christianity, the charter of the Christian Church, the only authoritative code of ecclesiastical law, and the warrant and justification of all Christian institutions. In it alone is life and immortality brought to light, the way of escape from wrath revealed, and all things necessary to salvation made plain; while its messages are a gospel of peace on earth and of hope to a lost world.
>
> Every man by nature possesses the right of private judgment in the interpretation of the Scriptures, and in all religious concerns; it is his privilege to read and explain the Bible for himself, without dictation from, or dependence on, any one, being responsible to God alone for his use of the sacred truth.
>
> Every man has the right to hold such religious opinions as he believes the Bible teaches, without harm or hindrance from any one on that account, so long as he does not intrude upon, or interfere with, the rights of others by so doing.
>
> All men have the right, not only to believe, but also to profess and openly declare, whatever religious opinions they may entertain, providing they be not contrary to common morality, and do no injustice to others.
>
> All men possess the common right to worship God according to the teachings of the Scriptures, as they understand them, without hindrance or molestation, so long as they do not injure or interfere with the rights of others by so doing.[2]

In the matter of relationship to the state, Baptists have established themselves by creed and practice to be the most patriotic and law-abiding of all citizens. That obedience is established by God's Word and limited by it. In the remaining statements on this matter Hiscox says:

> Civil governments, rulers and magistrates are to be respected, and in all temporal matters, not contrary to conscience and the word of God, to be obeyed; but they have no jurisdiction in spiritual concerns, and have no right of dictation to, of control over, or of intereference with, matters of religion; but are bound to protect all good citizens in the peaceable enjoyment of their religious rights and privileges.
>
> No organic union of Church and State should be tolerated, but entire separation maintained: the Church should neither ask for, nor accept of, support from civil authority, since to do so would imply the right of civil dictation and control. The support of religion belongs to those who profess it.
>
> Christian men are to be good and law-abiding citizens, sustaining and defending the government under which they live, in all things not contrary to conscience and the word of God; while such government is bound to protect them in the full enjoyment of all their rights and privileges, both civil and religious.
>
> Religion is to be free and voluntary, both as to faith, worship and service; neither conformity to, nor support of, religion in any form, should be compulsory. Christian faith and practice are matters of conscience and personal choice, and not subject to official dictation; and for either civil or ecclesiastical authority to enforce conformity, punish dissent, or compel the support of any form of worship, is a crime against the rights of man, an assumption of divine prerogatives, and treason against Christ, the only Lord of the conscience and sovereign of the soul.[3]

These statements have been the accepted view of Baptists. It is not unjust to say that, in the main, the heart of the faith stands on these Biblical tenets. There is no intention to move to the right or left even if the cost of holding them is prison and death.

God's holy Word is to be obeyed. It speaks, and the voice of believers echo. The state will have *no* jurisdiction, *no* right of dictation, *no* control, *no* interference in spiritual matters. The government is bound to protect righteous citizens.

When the church fails, however, to maintain this standard at all costs, the protection will also be lost. Without a question we presently see the rise of state violation in all of these areas. To understand where we are, and where we are going, a historical overview is necessary.

Born in Persecution

History records the conflict that ranges from a civil dictatorship to an ecclesiastical dictatorship. The church was born in persecution, and from its beginning the "blood of martyrs was the seed of the church."

> And Saul was consenting unto his death. And at that time there was a great persecution against the church which was at Jerusalem; and they were all scattered abroad throughout the regions of Judaea and Samaria, except the apostles.
>
> And devout men carried Stephen to his burial, and made great lamentation over him.
>
> As for Saul, he made havock of the church, entering into every house, and haling men and women committed them to prison.
>
> Therefore they that were scattered abroad went every where preaching the word (Acts 8:1-4).

The character of the saints in the New Testament church is incredible. Unlike the majority of Christians today, who would rather not fight, they died by the thousands because they refused to own any other Lord than Christ.

The detail of such dedication is given in many books. Among them is *Foxe's Christian Martyrs of the World.*

> But persecution could not diminish the ever-increasing flow of converts. It served, indeed, to make their numbers greater, for, to the Christian, death was but the beginning of eternal happiness. They therefore welcomed it almost with joy, and the sight of their cheerful countenances as they were led to execution, astonished the lookers-on, and made many inquire what this belief could be that seemed to rob death of its terrors. Thus a desire was awakened in hundreds of troubled hearts to share in the consolations which the new faith afforded believers.
>
> Many of those who lost their lives were men distinguished for their zeal and ability in spreading the gospel.[4]

To assume that the persecution of the New Testament church during the first three centuries was purely a state direction is error. There was adequate religious input by groups who wished to use the state to support their own constituency. This included the Judaizers identified in the New Testament Epistles and followers of pagan gods. A dual opposition created a colossal obstacle for the true church that, from the beginning, did not wish to violate the genuine claim of the state or the Word of God.

Conditions for those Christians were often beyond the comprehension of those of us who have never known such pressure.

> It is, of course, obvious that the conditions under which the Christian society was first developed made this distinction between the Church and the State obvious and even paramount in its experience. For, as we have observed before, for some three hundred years the Christian Church was not merely separate from the Roman State, but was continually in violent opposition to it.[5]

Cruelty of Rome

One would not stretch the point in emphasizing the cruelty of Rome. Its impatience was poured out in torture, imprisonment and extinction. However, the question is, Why was the church treated this way? Francis A. Schaeffer adequately answers this question.

> Rome was cruel, and its cruelty can perhaps be best pictured by the events which took place in the arena in Rome itself. People seated above the arena floor watched gladiator contests and Christians thrown to the beasts. Let us not forget why the Christians were killed. They were *not* killed because they worshiped Jesus. Various religions covered the whole Roman world. One such was the cult of Mithras, a popular Persian form of Zoroastrianism which had reached Rome by 67 B.C. Nobody cared who worshiped whom so long as the worshiper did not disrupt the unity of the state, centered in the formal worship of Caesar. The reason the Christians were killed was because they were rebels.[6]

Schaeffer goes on to say that this rebellion was based in their source of authority. They could not and would not accept the addition of state worship to the worship of Christ. He alone was their Master and He alone was Head of the church. This confrontation is further clarified.

> We may express the nature of their rebellion in two ways, both of which are true. First, we can say they worshiped Jesus as God and they worshiped the infinite-personal God only. The Caesars would not tolerate this worshiping of the one God *only*. It was counted as treason. Thus their worship became a special

> threat to the unity of the state during the third century and during the reign of Diocletian (284-305), when people of the higher classes began to become Christians in larger numbers. If they had worshiped Jesus *and* Caesar, they would have gone unharmed, but they rejected all forms of syncretism. They worshiped the God who had revealed himself in the Old Testament, through Christ, and in the New Testament which had gradually been written. And they worshiped Him as the *only* God. They allowed no mixture: All other gods were seen as false gods.
>
> We can only express in a second way why the Christians were killed: No totalitarian authority nor authoritarian state can tolerate those who have an absolute by which to judge that state and its actions. The Christians had that absolute in God's revelation. Because the Christians had an absolute, universal standard by which to judge not only personal morals but the state, they were counted as enemies of totalitarian Rome and were thrown to the beasts.[7]

Christians were viewed as outlaws. It was not a question of being religious. Christianity was viewed in a unique light. Other religions were allowed to continue but . . .

> To be a Christian was automatically a crime. Other religions were given official permission to exist and were thus made legal. The Church was an illegal faith. It was therefore in the power of the government to arrest a Christian and punish him whenever it saw fit.[8]

The state's reason for this is further stated.

> Always, however, the danger hung over Christian heads: at any moment the government might act. Many a Roman governor must have been tempted to use his power against the Church. For, like every government that conquers a vast empire and rules it by force, the Romans feared secret societies among the people. Was this illegal brotherhood called the Church really loyal to the Empire—especially since its members refused to swear by Caesar as a god?[9]

While our present situation has not arrived at torture and death, it has come to litigation and imprisonment. The church can have little doubt about what will happen next. A system that can subsidize the killing of infants and discuss the prospect of euthanasia has the capacity to crush religious dissenters in any way it pleases.

State Religion

This conflict with the state appeared to be over with the supposed conversion of Constantine in A.D. 312.

> Constantine treated Christianity as the favoured, though not yet the official, religion of the Empire. He granted immunities to the clergy and lavished gifts on the church; in his letters and edicts he spoke as if the Christian God were his own.[10]

But Constantine, who retained the pagan high priest's title as Pontifex Maximus, did no favor for the church. The church of the persecution had grown with a supernatural power. It also remained pure because of the cost of being a Christian. The identification of the church with the state brought a pseudo-growth and a fall from purity. By the end of the century it was a religion of the empire, but the cost was overwhelming.

> The Christian church took over many pagan ideas and images. From sun-worship, for example, came the celebration of Christ's birth on the twenty-fifth of December, the birthday of the sun. *Saturnalia,* the Roman winter festival of 17-21 of December, provided the merriment, gift-giving and candles typical of later Christmas holidays. Sun-worship hung on in Roman Christianity and Pope Leo I, in the middle of the fifth century, rebuked worshippers who turned round to bow to the sun before entering St. Peter's basilica. Some pagan customs which were later Christianized, for example the use of candles, incense and garlands, were at first avoided by the church because they symbolized paganism.[11]

As Constantine wedded the church and state, a terrible power began to develop. The emperor felt obligated to protect the church, purify it from paganism, repress rash indiscretion. His sons outdid their father in an attack on paganism and heresy. But what followed was an establishment of a state church that would not tolerate true Christianity.

A Persecuting Church

From the church that was persecuted we moved to the church as the persecutor, the Holy Catholic Church.

> Until Christianity conquered the Caesars and became the religion of the Roman State, it had been often persecuted, but never a persecutor. As if to show that this was merely because it had lacked the power, as if to prove that in this respect the religion of the Christ was no better than the religions of the gods that it displaced, the Holy Catholic Church almost immediately began to persecute, thereby affording a convincing demonstration that it was neither catholic nor holy. Indeed, persecution was an inevitable consequence of the union of Church and State under Constantine; no other result could reasonably have been looked for, with the confusion of civil and ecclesiastical rights that followed the promotion of Christianity to be a State religion.[12]

With the power of a state religion, opposing religious views were quickly dismissed. As the pendulum passed to the side of the established church, the state ceased to be the cooperative of the church. Government was established as the tool and servant of the Roman Church. This meant a crushing of all religious dissidents, and this state church fell with fury upon the legitimate New Testament church that existed outside the Catholic church.

It is my opinion that a true body of believers always existed outside the state church. No purging, inquisition, persecution or oppression could crush it.

The period that followed is a black one for the state church. It is a glorious record of dozens of groups and their brave leaders.

> The truth was never quite crushed to earth; there were always parties or sects, bitterly hated and persecuted by Catholics, that held with more or less consistency to the evangelical religion. These comparatively pure survivals are found latest in the two extreme portions of the then civilized Europe, in Britain and in Bulgaria.[13]

Among the dissidents was Patrick, born around A.D. 360, but it was not until the eleventh century that men like Arnold began to openly defy the state church. He was hanged by the prefect and burned, his ashes scattered over the Tiber. Girolamo Savonarola (born in 1452) was hanged by the papal power. Still four hundred years remained until the successful challenge came to Rome. We must note that Savonarola was not really a heretic. He believed in the church dogmas even at his death. His real conflict with the pope was a political one. However, the state church would not tolerate even these dissidents.

The Reformers

One hundred years before Luther, John Hus came preaching the doctrines of John Wycliffe. At first, Hus was interested in reforming the church from within. He was excommunicated in March 1411, but paid no attention, and with his sympathizers openly taught that the pope and his lackeys had no right to draw the sword. This was a serious charge to the Roman Church that had become drunk with the blood of saints and her own dissidents.

Hus was summoned to appear before the ecumenical council under safe conduct. A month of hearings followed, and on July 6, 1415, he was condemned. The church then delivered him to the civil power for execution, and he was burned at the stake. The hypocrisy here exhibited is found in the fact that the church ruled the state. No civil government was ever given the power of capital punishment for heresy.

His death was a terrible mistake for Rome. The followers of Hus, the Hussites, spread to the Bohemian Brethren and later to the Moravians. When Luther came on the scene, four hundred of their churches were in existence. However, the power of Rome did not change through the separatist movements.

It is the basic purpose of this chapter only to give an overview of the church-state struggle. This is done without effort to judge the character or beliefs of those mentioned. Touching history here and there, one man cannot be ignored. The title "Father of the Reformation" has been given to Martin Luther. It is imperative to note some things about him.

Like Hus, it was his direction to reform the church from within. It is also important to note that Luther confessed to holding views similar to Hus.

> They had this singular effect upon Luther: they drove him to see that his Augustinian views were identical with those of Wyclif and Huss [sic]. He was astonished, as he described it, to find that 'he was a Hussite without knowing it; that St. Paul and Augustine were Hussites!'
>
> The fact was that Wyclif and Huss [sic], like Luther, had in a great degree got their views from the works of St. Augustine:

they had so adopted many of the doctrines which belonged to what we have said is now called the *Calvinistic* theology.[14]

Luther was peasant born and never forgot it. He was classified as an angry man and was known for outburst and conflict. No one with a mind for fairness would criticize his dedication and sincerity. It was this combination of characteristics that made him a reformer as recorded in *Valiant for the Faith.*

> *Who can describe this mountain of a man, this human kaleidoscope, this composite of a hundred contrasting colors? At once rough and tender, poet and pugilist, boisterous and devout, deadly serious and yet possessor of a Falstaffian wit, unrelenting enemy and steadfast friend, exquisitely sensitive in hymnody and volcanic in invective, bold before men, humble before God—this begins to describe the Reformer of Saxony.*[15]

History taught this outspoken theological explorer that to defy the state church brings sure death. Safe conduct and any other pledge of the papal representative was worthless. With one last appeal, with every ounce of conviction at the Diet of Worms, he attacked the doctrines of Roman error and replied:

> "Except I can be convinced by clear and conclusive reasoning, or by proofs taken from the Holy Scriptures, I neither can nor will recant, because it is neither safe nor advisable to do anything which is against my conscience. Here I stand. I cannot do otherwise, so help me God! Amen."[16]

On April 26, 1521, he departed Worms under a strong escort. On his journey home he was spirited away by his friends, who took him to the castle of Wartburg near Eisenach. This act was the plan of the Elector of Saxony, who wished to protect him from the wrath of the pope. When the pontiff discovered he might be yet alive, he sought to take his life and destroy his writings. Luther's reply was, ". . . If they burn me and all my books; the people are now in possession of the Holy Scriptures. . . ."[17]

No fair-minded man will demean the good work of this reformer either, yet his record is stained by some things. Let us note one of them.

Luther's Failure

One would surely think that Luther's conflict with the state church and his discovery of the Scriptures would have led him to choose against church power. He had produced a movement in Germany which was able to withstand political and ecclesiastical power. Opportunity for freedom could now come to all religious groups. However, he failed in this prime point, as recorded by A. H. Newman.

> *The maintenance of the union of Church and State* was the most vicious point in Luther's system. As the uniting of Church and State had done more than all other influences combined to corrupt the church, and as this union always furnished the most unyielding obstacle to reform, so its retention by Luther made it absolutely impossible that any thorough reformation of the Church should find place.[18]

Luther was less than kind to those who did not agree with his doctrine. His lifelong fight with Rome left him a soured man. Even the relationship of friends was clouded with gloom in his last days. His conflict with the Anabaptists and followers of Zwingli and Calvin was less than charitable. Sadly enough, his recommendation for the retention and destruction of these individuals resounded of church power that entered the civil realm.

Anabaptists as Separatists

On the other hand, the Anabaptists, through their suffering, had learned something. A small light began to shine for the separation of church and state. While this practice of separation did not become a major reality until the American dream, it is said of them:

> They repudiated absolutely any sort of connection between Church and State, regarding the State as an institution outside of and apart from the gospel of Christ, whose authority was to be obeyed in all things lawful, but which had no right to interfere in matters of conscience. Hence also the doctrine of absolute liberty of conscience was a fundamental tenet of the Anabaptists as it had been of the mediaeval evangelicals.
>
> In consistency with their views on Church and State, they denied the right of a Christian to exercise magistracy, which seemed to them to involve a violation of Christ's precept and example. Christ refused to sit in judgment in the dispute of the two brothers regarding an inheritance, and he contrasted the kings of the earth who exercised lordship with the humility of his disciples whose Master had not where to lay his head.[19]

The tie to the state remained in the European countries. Even in England freedom was not to be found. The struggle continues to this day; a church state in the Scandanavian countries and England, but nowhere, in a pure sense, can we find the separation of the two, as equal powers.

Since the launching pad for the American dream was England, we need a brief view of the problem there. Not one doubt is left in our minds; people came to America for religious freedom. An oppressive state is as evil as an oppressive state church. The latter may be more ruthless because of its knowledge of the separatists and the insults that the dissident's existence heaped upon its reputation.

Puritan Movement

The word *puritan* explains the purpose of this group. They desired to "purify" the Church of England. Much of the Catholic corruption remained in the established English Church. Nonconformists disliked the vestments of the clergy and held to the priesthood of believers. The Lord's Supper to them was a memorial, and they disliked the form of government in the church. These many areas of disagreement were not the real source of the problem. Parliament passed acts in 1593 that named the Puritans as seditious sectaries and disloyal persons.

> Even more radical were the Separatists or Independents. The Puritans wished to remain within the Church of England and to have it, cleansed according to their patterns, as the religious wing of the nation's life to which all the queen's subjects would belong. In contrast, the Separatists or Independents, like the Anabaptists on the Continent, believed in "gathered" churches, not made up of all the inhabitants of a particular area, but only of those who were consciously Christian. They were to be united with one another and with Christ in a covenant. Each congregation so united, with Christ as its head, was a self-governing church which elected its own pastor and other officers after what was believed to be the pattern discernible in the New Testament. No church was to have authority over any other and in each church every member was responsible for the welfare of the whole and of his fellow-members. In theory and to a large extent in practice, such churches were pure democracies. They were the spiritual ancestors of the later Congregationalists. They were Separatists in that they withdrew from the Church of England and were Independents in that they

believed in the full autonomy of each local church. They were not Anabaptists.[20]

Another example of state church power is exhibited in the decree of 1622 when . . .

James sought (1622) to restrict preachers to topics which seemed to him non-controversial and forbade them to deal with predestination or matters of state or to rail at "either Papists or Puritans," an obvious attempt to curb both Puritans and their opponents.[21]

A frightening picture of state power over the church is painted in the Act of Supremacy passed by Parliament in 1534.

The king our sovereign lord, his heirs and successors, kings of this realm, shall be taken, accepted, and reputed the only supreme head on earth of the Church of England, . . . and shall have and enjoy, annexed and united to the imperial crown of this realm, as well the title and style thereof, as all honors, dignities, preeminences, jurisdictions, privileges, authorities, immunities, profits, and commodities to the said dignity of supreme head of the same church belonging and appertaining; and that our said sovereign lord, his heirs, and successors, . . . shall have full authority and power from time to time to visit, refer, redress, reform, order, correct, restrain, and amend all such errors, heresies, abuses, offenses, contempt, enormities, whatsoever they be, which by any spiritual authority and jurisdiction ought or may lawfully be reformed, . . . any usage, custom, foreign law, foreign authority, prescription, or any other thing or things to the contrary notwithstanding.

This act is further so defined as to give to the king absolute ecclesiastical authority alike in matters external (church order, revenues, bestowing of benefices, etc.), and in matters internal (the repression of false doctrine and the promotion of true, etc.).

Cromwell, already keeper of the great seal, was now, though a layman, made vicar-general of the church. Bishops and clergy were speedily brought into a condition of utter subserviency. Not only were their ecclesiastical duties in general prescribed, but the time, subject, and subject-matter of their discourses as well. Spies were generally on hand to report the slightest deviation from instructions and the merest hints at dissatisfaction with the government.[22]

John Bunyan

Let us briefly view an illustration of religious violation. His name was John Bunyan. The state had told him plainly it was against the law not to attend the approved church. Since he was viewed as an unlicensed preacher, he was held in breach of the peace and further, branded as ignorant of the original languages and unable to understand the Scriptures. In his literal interpretation they said he was a hindrance to the common people. Several of the justice's servants begged him to be "reasonable." Bunyan was convinced, however, that Christ was in control, not the state.

> So we have the famous trial-scene in the old chantry Chapel of Herne which did duty for a shire hall in Bunyan's Bedford. It was at the January Quarter Sessions, 1661. The Sessions Chairman was Sir John Kelynge, later to draw up the new Act of Uniformity, and now within five years of his appointment as Lord Chief Justice.
>
> Again the observable fact is that Bunyan was taken seriously. He was charged with having "devilishly and perniciously abstained from coming to church to hear Divine service" and with being "a common upholder of several unlawful meetings and conventicles to the great disturbance and distraction of the good subjects of this kingdom." But after a perfunctory question or two from the Bench ("Do you come to church—you know what I mean—to the parish church—to hear Divine service?"), Kelynge found himself "at a point" with this tall raw-boned man with his "quick eyes," commanding countenance and mop of rusty hair; and not simply so, but curiously interested as well, and drawn into a strange discussion. For in fact, as we know, the trial developed into nothing more than a lengthy and animated conversation between the two—a thing curious enough to behold and to hear, and plainly displeasing to some of the purple-faced country-gentry on the Bench.[23]

Bunyan was a master in the use of the English language. His accusers called him an ignorant man, but we hardly know any of their names. If they could speak or write we do not know, but John could.

> *One would expect him to be a Nonconformist, and he was. Because he insisted on conducting services not recognized by the Church of England, the authorities sentenced him to a twelve-year term of imprisonment. With only the*

> *Bible, a copy of Fox's* Book of Martyrs, *and a rich and lively imagination, Bunyan commenced putting together his immortal works.*[24]

He lived sixteen years after his release from prison and, of course, in the main, spent his time with Baptist communions. Those nonconformist views were only made stronger by the walls of the Bedford prison.

Before we cross the sea with the Puritans we would remind ourselves that England never did make right her wrong. Robert W. Dale who was born in 1829 lamented the power of the church law.

> Dale caught something of this spirit. Though less detached from human affairs, he was impelled by the religious motive. He too was wont to appeal to the higher and nobler elements in human character, and instinctively avoided those mean and petty issues by which a great controversy is too often degraded. He, like his leader, believed with his whole heart that in attacking the position of the Established Church, Nonconformists must aim, not so much to right themselves as to right Christianity. But he was very far from Miall's individualism. Miall's supreme interest lay in God on the one hand, in the individual soul on the other. "Compared with them, all institutions, whether secular or sacred, were insignificant. Nations and churches existed for the sake of individual man." In Dale's thought the Church and the nation held a higher place. He considered them to be essential, not secondary. And attaching, as he did, the highest importance to the true conception of the Church and its functions, he contended against the maintenance of a national church, because in his view it stood in the way of the true idea of the Church; and only as that idea prevailed had he any hope of the nation becoming Christian in reality as well as in name.
>
> He believed, therefore, that if Christianity were to exert its full power over the English people—not for civilisation but for conversion—the Church as by law established must cease to be.[25]

England has never fully corrected her violation. The conflict continued, and it brought the American dream to reality: a wall of separation between church and state. However, as late as the close of the 1800s some still hoped for a new direction in England.

> Steadily though slowly through long years, marked but by

few observers, yet of late with a rapidity that has attracted all eyes, the great question of the relation of the Church to the State has been coming to the fore, until even the careless and reluctant have to confess that it has become the question of the day. It is likely to continue such for many a day to come. It refuses to be remanded to the domain of intellectual controversy, among the shadowy crowd of abstract speculations. It comes into court as a practical, real, living problem, putting in a claim which can no longer be evaded, to be earnestly dealt with, and wisely, justly, finally settled. Men see—some with hope, as the mariner who sights from the masthead the white cliffs within whose sheltering embrace lie his haven and his home; others with terror, as one whose vessel feels the outer curve of the whirlpool—that changes are at hand in England, whether wise or foolish, for good or for evil, the sum total of which will amount to an ecclesiastical revolution, greater, it may be, than the Reformation itself.[26]

Footnotes

1. Edward T. Hiscox, *The New Directory for Baptist Churches* (Valley Forge, PA: Judson Press, 1894; reprint ed., Grand Rapids: Kregel Publications, 1970), p. 11.
2. Ibid., pp. 11, 12.
3. Ibid., pp. 12, 13.
4. John Foxe, *Foxe's Christian Martyrs of the World* (Chicago: Moody Press, n.d.), pp. 42, 43. Used by permission.
5. A. J. Carlyle, *The Christian Church and Liberty* (New York: George H. Doran Co., 1924), p. 79.
6. Francis A. Schaeffer, *How Should We Then Live?* (Old Tappan, NJ: Fleming H. Revell Co., 1976), p. 24.
7. Ibid., pp. 24, 26.
8. Norman F. Langford, *Fire Upon the Earth* (Philadelphia: The Westminster Press, 1940), p. 31.
9. Ibid.
10. Tim Dooley, ed., *Eerdman's Handbook to the History of Christianity* (Grand Rapids: Wm. B. Eerdmans Publishing Co., 1977), p. 131. Used by permission.
11. Ibid., pp. 131, 132.
12. Henry C. Vedder, *A Short History of the Baptists* (Valley Forge, PA: Judson Press, 1907), p. 95.

13. Ibid., p. 71.

14. Frederic Seebohm, "The Era of the Protestant Revolution," Edward E. Morris, ed., series on *Epochs of History,* No. 1 (New York: Scribner Armstrong and Co., 1874), p. 106.

15. David Otis Fuller, ed., *Valiant for the Truth* (New York: McGraw-Hill Book Co., 1961), p. 117.

16. Martin Luther, *Epistle to the Galatians* (Philadelphia: Salmon S. Miles, 1840), p. 47.

17. Ibid., p. 48.

18. Albert Henry Newman, *A Manual of Church History,* Vol. II (Valley Forge, PA: Judson Press, 1902), p. 119.

19. Ibid., p. 154.

20. Kenneth Scott Latourette, *A History of Christianity* (New York: Harper & Brothers, 1953), p. 815.

21. Ibid., pp. 817, 818.

22. Albert Henry Newman, p. 258.

23. Gwilym O. Griffith, *John Bunyan* (London: Hodder & Stoughton, 1927), pp. 136, 137.

24. Fuller, p. 222.

25. A. W. W. Dale, *The Life of R. W. Dale of Birmingham* (London: Hodder & Stoughton, 1898), pp. 369, 370.

26. Eustace Rogers Conder, "The Relation of the Church to the State," in *Ecclesia: Church Problems Considered,* Henry Robert Reynolds, ed. (London: Hodder & Stoughton, 1870), p. 195.

FOUR

The American Dream

"They were patriotic to the core; but as the war cloud darkened, they agreed to promote the common cause on condition that they be allowed to worship God in their own way, without interruption; that they be permitted to maintain their own ministers and no others; that they be married or buried without paying the clergy of other denominations" (T. J. Villers).

SOME MAY FEEL that limiting the record of a successful separation of church and state to America is extreme. It is true, however, and there was a specific reason for it. In the main, those who came to the new world did so to escape oppression. The English Puritan Separatist first went to Holland. This was not a permanent answer. In 1620 the trip to America commenced, and after many setbacks the Mayflower carried them to Plymouth. Here they set in order their first government under the "Mayflower Compact."

Escaping Persecution

Not everyone who came to the new colony did so for religious reasons. We maintain, however, that this was, in the main, the basic purpose of the immigration. When persecution was on the rise in England in 1630, many thousands came to the new world. They settled from Maine to the islands off Florida. Those who came for freedom also sought opportunity.

> It has been claimed that one of the most powerful side-effects of the Reformation was to give oppressed people a spiritual motive for emigration. The first colonists combined missionary zeal with a desire for freedom of worship; at the same time they certainly had commercial motives too.
>
> Successive waves of immigrants from Britain and Europe came to the east coast. All but one of the thirteen English colonies had Protestant beginnings, and it was here that the Great Awakening occurred.[1]

One must note that we record the arrival of immigrants listed as Calvinists, Dutch Reformed, Puritans, Dunkers, Lutherans, Moravians and Mennonites, to name a few. The answer to the question, "Why the religious identification?" is simply that the movement to the new world was religious in nature and in number.

A Dream or a Nightmare?

Then the American dream almost became a nightmare. The great Massachusetts Bay settlement failed to establish a separation of civil power. Plymouth was swept in the same direction. In one of the finest current books on the subject, *Baptists and the American Tradition,* Robert Newman spells out the tragedy.

> Thus, it was again a religious migration with a commercial base. These Boston Puritans were not only greater in number than their brethren in Plymouth, but also different in kind. Like the Plymouth group, they were Calvinists, congregationalists in church government and believers in a strong regenerate church membership—one which would control the political affairs of the colony. They accomplished this by restricting officeholding and voting privileges to the church member, thereby disenfranchising a large portion of the populace. In one respect they differed from Plymouth. They believed in the Anglican way. . . .[2]

What happened in the migration was a move of the state and church from the old land to the new. A new kind of oppression now existed: a church state. Religious freedom meant they could believe what they wished, and everyone else was required to believe and practice what they wished as long as it agreed with the established church.

> Plymouth and Massachusetts were really not so far apart as they had thought, for by 1691 the two colonies merged. In both, the Congregational Church held sway and religion was tolerated only if one went their way. . . .

And then:

> To summarize the early colonial background, in all except three colonies some form of a practical church-state union held sway, and religious uniformity was the usual picture. In New England and Virginia it was strongest. Some measure of religious diversity began to creep in by way of the Middle Colonies, due to diversified settlers. For the most part, however, only in three colonies were a large and open degree of religious toleration and church-state separation attempted. In Maryland a good beginning, while begun out of economic rather than religious scruple, soon wasted away until the established church was Anglican. Only in Rhode Island and Pennsylvania would an open spirit of toleration, a freedom from religious persecution and a stated and practiced church-state separation be maintained from its founding, on through the Revolution and up to the disestablishment period. . . .[3]

One more quote from this fine work will help set the direction for our major illustration and the building of the successful foundation for the wall of separation.

> Since the Rhode Island Experiment in religious freedom is one of the chief interests of this volume, we simply note here that it was one of three colonial attempts in liberty, and move quickly to "Penn's Woods." William Penn (1644-1718), London-born, was an ardent follower of George Fox and his Quaker movement. Expelled in 1661 from Christ Church, Oxford, for his Nonconformist views, he served briefly in the English Navy and studied law in London. Penn was imprisoned several times for his nonconformity. These occasions allowed time for writing. After his marriage in 1672, he helped eight hundred Quakers secure a footing in New Jersey (1677-78).[4]

Had the Massachusetts Bay Colony been all there was to the character of American religion, the separation principle would never have become a reality. These were Puritans who wanted the church changed, but they were not Separatists.

New England Puritanism. During the early years of Charles' reign, thousands of Puritans emigrated to New England, having secured charters more liberal than such a ruler might have been expected to grant. In 1628 a colony of nonconforming Puritans settled at Salem, Mass. It was largely reinforced in 1629. A far larger and more important colony was planted in 1629 on Massachusetts Bay, which in a few years had several thousand members, including such leaders as Winthrop, Saltonstall, Dudley, Noel, Johnson, and Pynchon, and was soon equipped with such highly educated ministers as John Cotton, Hugh Peter, Thomas Hooker, John Wilson, and Richard Mather.

The Massachusetts Bay colonists claimed to be loyal church men and esteemed it an honor to call the Church of England their dear mother. Even the Salem men declined to be regarded as Separatists; but they were soon brought by the influence of the Plymouth colonists and the force of circumstances to such pronounced Separatism that they would not administer the ordinances to members of the Massachusetts Bay Colony because they belonged to no reformed church. The Massachusetts Bay colonists soon became as pronounced as any in their opposition to the forms and ceremonies of the English church and proceeded to establish a theocracy like that of Geneva, in which citizenship was made dependent on fellowship in a church, fellowship in a church on a personal profession of saving faith, and the validity of a church organization on the sanction of the church already organized.[5]

Roger Williams

Into this bizarre situation came Roger Williams. After his wedding to Mary Barnhard in 1629, the couple migrated to Massachusetts. Even before his departure, affiliation with the Separatists was a foregone conclusion.

There were probably many different factors which brought about Roger's decision to emigrate to Massachusetts. He realized, for one thing, that he had put himself into a ludicrous position so far as Lady Barrington was concerned, and the fact that he had married her granddaughter only made the matter more embarrassing. Too, Roger was not inclined to throw in his lot with those who were loyal to the crown: instead he found his sympathies moving in the direction of those who held that the Crown should be completely dissociated from the Church and the Church altogether independent of the Crown.

The recent pronouncements of Archbishop Laud were

> especially distasteful to him. The archbishop had been particularly stern in his denunciation of Separatists and Roger was inclined to accept their point of view regarding government and the Church. He was well aware, of course, that the Separatists were of many different minds. Among them were those who were eager to cut off all ties with the Church of England or else reconstitute the Church with the abolition of the bishopric and liturgy. Included in this group were those who called themselves Independents or Congregationalists. To their way of thinking each individual church should be autonomous.[6]

He arrived in Boston Harbor to the greeting of Governor John Winthrop, who invited him to take charge of conducting the services at Boston Church. The trip from England had evidently been a time of serious reflection for him. The Separatist views he had pondered became solidified. The entire church organization was wrong and it should not be tied to the Crown. "To make the church subservient to the Crown was to place the Crown above the church. It was tantamount to demeaning God."[7]

What followed was the very key to the establishment of the separation of powers. Roger was awarded the position of teacher by vote of the magistrates, but he refused to enter into the agreement. To add insult to injury, the prospective minister declared that God would not permit him to officiate at an unseparated church. The offended governor demanded an explanation. Williams boldly declared that the church and civil government should be separate. To show what a failure the Massachusetts colony had been in this area, a surprised magistrate replied that the union of the church and civil affairs was established in the homeland as well as in the new land and the two were inseparable. Standing on the Word of God and the example of Christ, Roger outlined their error. Magistrates and the people were in an uproar.

From the beginning these views were seen as heretical. Not because they offended the Bible, but because they offended the established church. Winthrop's reply is a revealing statement.

> "You have gone too far," he explained. "Perhaps some day a colony will be formed in which the principles which you have enunciated will become the rule by which the people who populate it will run their affairs—but this was not the time nor the place to set them forth. We have a mixed population here. There are those among our colonists who are exceedingly pious, good folk, who sought to find in this new land an opportunity

to found a settlement in which they could live free from the sins of society in the mother country. On the other hand, we have those hardy adventurers who have little or no respect for the conventions of others. They blaspheme openly. They jeer at the church and, of course, they do not attend its services. These must be made to see the error of their ways."

"The way to correct them, then, is not by civil law," Roger objected. "The only means of correction which should be employed is the example of godly folk. Believe me, Mr. Winthrop, I do not condone Sabbath-breaking nor swearing. My point is that these are not violations of civil law. Hence their violation does not fall within the purview of the magistrate's function."[8]

From this original encounter Williams's views were well-known. The result was that no place was open to him except Plymouth, which was not under the economic or political power of the Massachusetts Bay Colony. Roger and Mary walked to Plymouth living from hand to mouth. As a preacher he was invited to teach a Bible class and he did so. The couple joined the little church inasmuch as it was not under the control of ecclesiastical authority and its form of government was congregational.

True to Roger's conclusion, this community of people was free to attend or not attend. They were not punished for religious crimes. Their response was one of pure devotion. We are reminded that all of these people came from England under persecution. They were a different breed of colonist. It appears that civil disputes were settled by the town council, and church matters settled in the congregation.

Williams was appointed to the post of assistant pastor. Shortly after, they were visited by Pastor John Wilson, Governor Winthrop and a delegation from Boston. The subject of the meetings was Williams's departure from orthodoxy. The week-long confab ended with a friendly farewell.

The pulpit assertions of this outspoken man soon brought several difficult situations. Governor Bradford of Plymouth handled them well with the help of Mary, who also was annoyed by her husband's controversies. By the year 1634, Roger and several members who agreed with him left the community for Salem. His writings there precipitated more turmoil. The result was a call to appear in the court of Boston. Things could be tolerated, but the demand that church and state be separated was incredible.

"Honorable magistrates," Roger began, "I have come before you previously to express my views on questions of

> tremendous import to the welfare of both the Colony and the Church. I am as firmly convinced as ever that the court does not have and should not have jurisdiction of the souls of men. I am equally certain that in a court of law no unregenerate person should be allowed to take an oath before giving his testimony, and then affirming said oath by the phrase, 'So help me God.' If such a person does not believe in God how can he . . ."[9]

He was interrupted and not allowed to proceed. When asked to recant he refused; hence the court banished the troublesome man from its jurisdiction.

Banished

The court did Williams, his followers and the future nation a favor. He temporarily left Mary and their first child at Salem. Upon the advice of Governor Winthrop, who continued to befriend him, he went to the area of Narragansett Bay. On a cold January day, Williams and Thomas Angell set out on a journey that would set the pace for the Separatists.

The events that followed are not as important as the accomplishment of his life spelled out by John Garrett.

> America has come to think of Williams as a banished man. The magistrates of Boston certainly expelled him from their jurisdictions by order of their general court in October 1635. Yet long before, his friends in England had loved his honesty and hated his impetuous ways. "Divinely mad," they called him. It is a good description as long as the accent is on the adverb. In looking into his letters and books to find his secret one discovers a Calvinist Puritan who became a runaway and preferred the rough wilderness of dissent to the tidy gardens of the conventional clergy. The logic of his banishment is prefigured in the English society that brought him to young manhood. His understanding of the meaning of the Bible for the Church and its task in the world had radical implications for the state church systems of the older Christendom. His founding of the community of Rhode Island was a frontier experiment among wild men; but it held the seed within it for formal separation of church and state elsewhere.[10]

Quaker Quarrel

The settlement was established throughout Williams's life. He was a very strong leader. The ultimate question of this discourse now arises. What did Williams do with his view on separation when those in power agreed with him? The best example of this was the Quaker conflict.

George Fox, the leader of this group, was an unusual man. Many followed his views and were labeled fanatics. Their actions as well as their doctrines drew the anger of the established church.

> Quakers were imprisoned, sometimes thousands of them, for such offences as refusing to speak deferentially to judges, meeting in forbidden religious assembly, or refusing the compulsory state church tithe. If they were asked to take the oath in court, they refused on the basis of Jesus' words, 'Swear not at all . . .'
>
> In Boston, New England, a confrontation occurred between the Puritans who had left their homes in England to set up a pure Christian community and the Quakers who challenged their religious exclusiveness. When banishment failed to eliminate the Quakers, Governor Endicott ordered the death penalty. Three Quakers were hanged on Boston Common (1660-61) because they chose to hold their convictions rather than obey the authorities. Their deaths raised an outcry against intolerance which helped pave the way for religious liberty.[11]

The Quakers came to Rhode Island in 1657, but they remained an offense to Massachusetts. The government of Massachusetts wanted the Quakers controlled and suppressed. But here is the beginning of a bright light.

> Rhode Island declined, naturally, since permission of all consciences was fundamental to the terms of their original charter. Even though more sober magistrates in Rhode Island, particularly the better educated Baptists, may have disliked the teachings and immoderate enthusiasm of the Quakers, they had no intention of proceeding against them unless they defied decency or public order. Roger Williams was necessarily of the same mind; little could be done, short of public debate; for many years he refrained from doing battle on that front, probably because he was deeply involved already with prominent Quaker converts on other fronts.[12]

In due time an open debate raged between Williams and George Fox. The temperament of Roger Williams leads us to the conclusion that the battle was bitter, and it went on for many years. Fox, on the other hand, accused Williams of agreeing to the persecution of Quakers.

> A last relic in writing of the debates of 1672 is a rare item from the pen of George Fox called *Something in Answer to a Letter,* published in 1677. It is a reply to a letter written by Governor Leverett to William Coddington, "wherein he mentions my name, and also wherein John Leverett justifies Roger Williams's book of lies." Evidently Williams's book was by then in print, or possibly circulating in proof. In this pathetic little tract by Fox there are some poignant protests against the whipping of Quaker women at Boston. He cried out against such injustice—"to whip men and women till you cleaved the teats of their breasts (as you did Anne Coleman) . . . " He warned Leverett: "Herod and Pilate were made friends when they turned against Christ; and it's like you and Roger Williams are made friends in your turning against God's people and his truth now." In spite of the *non sequitur,* that because Williams chose to refute vehemently in speech and writing he was therefore in favour of physical persecution for religion, the small book shows Fox's love of the cause he embodied and his care for all its despised and hurt witnesses.[13]

Whatever he was guilty of, it does not appear Williams ever changed his view on the separation of powers. A course had been set for a new government free from religious intrusion.

Virginia's Struggle

It is not the purpose of this writing to deal with every influence that brought about a unique religious freedom. However, another illustration is in order, that of Virginia. In New England the Puritans had come, hopefully, to purify the Church of England from afar. In Virginia the established church was not concerned with the continuing reformation. The state church of Virginia presented another serious obstacle to the nonconformist.

> In New England the church dominated the state. In Virginia their roles were reversed. The New England magistrates were the "nursing fathers" to the church. They were charged with enforcing both "tables of the law" and with punishing schismatics. Beyond this, however, the Congregational Church was

> allowed a relatively free reign. The religious tax levied on the citizenry assured a sound financial base. It did not begin to give way until the late seventeenth century, and then only slowly.
>
> In Virginia, on the other hand, the state determined the progress of the church. True, Anglicanism was fully established. It was also fully controlled. Virginia's House of Burgesses decreed what the Church of England could and could not do, to a large measure at any rate. The established clergy held sole right to perform marriages and bury the dead. A dissenter had no choice but to use their services in these matters. Then, too, the church held large parcels of plebe lands bought at public expense and given to the establishment. The clergy was supported by a stipend system. Virginia was essentially a mercantile venture and its main commodity was in smoke—tobacco was king. Clerical salaries were in the form of stipends fixed by the law in pounds of tobacco, the crop being widely used as a currency in Virginia. Thus, while Anglican ministers were state supported, they were also state regulated. . . .[14]

The reason for the conflict with the state was the argument over its involvement in church offices. As early as 1738 John Caldwell petitioned Governor Gooch to extend the Act of Toleration toward those nonconformists who lived to the west of the Piedmont area. The Governor was kindly disposed to do so, thinking that there was no threat of contact with them. Two things changed the course of events. One was the great growth of these dissidents, made up of Baptists, Presbyterians and Methodists. The other was a series of revivals that swept their ranks.

Excitement among these revivalists was first ignored, then ridiculed. When the wave touched the established church of the Old Dominion, it was time for action. Civil authorities arrested some dissidents and fined them for non-attendance at the approved church. There is no question that attendance had fallen off at the parish churches. This was compounded by the problem that preachers such as John Roan, who was unlicensed, openly attacked the state church with what was considered to be abusive language.

> Governor Gooch viewed this conduct as a menace to public peace and order. In his charge to the grand jury in 1745, Gooch called attention to "certain false teachers that are lately crept into this government, who, without order or license, or producing any testimonial of their education or sect, professing themselves ministers under the pretended influence of new light, extraordinary impulses and such like satirical [fanatical?] and

enthusiastic knowledge, lead the ignorant and innocent people into all kinds of delusions."[15]

Roan, William Morris and others were fined for offending a civil-religious law. Conflict began to stir. Questions debated at this time centered around the laws requiring participation in the established church. This was understood to mean that only licensed congregations and ministers were acceptable.

Imprisoned

On June 4, 1768, John Waller, Lewis Craig, James Childs and other Baptist leaders were arrested and charged with disturbing the peace. In trial, the prosecutor complained about these evangelistic persons who ram Scripture down one's throat. The arrests became more frequent. Fortunately the dissidents had men such as Mason, Madison, Jefferson and Patrick Henry to champion their cause.

> In Virginia the importance of the issues raised by the arrest of the Baptist leaders was at once recognized by no less a leader than Patrick Henry who, hearing of the confinement of the Baptist preachers in the Spottsylvania jail, journeyed fifty miles to volunteer his services in their aid. The old Presbyterian historian Foote has given us the following description of Henry's part in the trial:
>
> "The King's attorney having made some remarks containing the indictment, Henry said—'May it please your worships, I think I heard read by the prosecutor, as I entered the house, the paper I now hold in my hand. If I have rightly understood, the king's attorney has framed an indictment for the purpose of arraigning, and punishing by imprisonment, these three inoffensive persons before the bar of this Court for a crime of great magnitude—as disturbers of the peace. May it please the Court, what did I hear read? Did I hear an expression, as of a crime, that these men, whom your worships are about to try for misdemeanor, are charged with,—with,—what?' Then in a low, solemn, heavy tone he continued—'preaching the gospel of the Son of God?' Pausing amid profound silence, he waved the paper three times around his head, then raising his eyes and hands to heaven, with peculiar and impressive energy, he exclaimed—'Great God!' A burst of feeling from the audience followed this exclamation."[16]

The magistrates made the same mistake as those religious civil rulers in the Acts of the Apostles. Persecuted preachers became heroes. In prison they continued to preach. When the authorities offered to let them go if they would be quiet, they refused. In the end, the authorities were unable to conquer such independent spirits.

There is no adequate record of the cruelty suffered or the number of those who died for the building of the wall of separation. In a pamphlet that every student should read, "Fidelity to Our Baptist Heritage," the words of T. J. Villers (edited by R. T. Ketcham) summarize this:

> A halo of glory will forever wreathe the name of Virginia Baptists, for they protested and petitioned, they struggled and suffered, till the principle of soul liberty was grafted into our national constitution. Virginia was settled by Cavaliers, whose charter of 1606 made the Episcopal faith the religion of the colony. Withdrawal from the Episcopal church was accounted a crime equal to revolt against the government. The charter provided that nonconformists should be arrested and imprisoned till fully and thoroughly reformed. The clergyman's salary was fixed at sixteen thousand pounds of tobacco. It was levied on the parish and collected like other taxes. Absence one Sunday from an Episcopal service was punished with a fine of fifty pounds of tobacco; absence for a month, four thousand pounds; refusal to have one's baby sprinkled, two thousand pounds. So that the support of Episcopacy in Virginia, as Doctor Carroll remarks, made "awful inroads on Baptist tobacco." Baptist ministers were fined, beaten, imprisoned, poisoned. Sometimes a snake or a hornet's nest was thrown into their meeting. Not infrequently the ordinance of baptism was rudely interrupted, the administrator and the candidate being held beneath the water till nearly drowned. . . .[17]

A Dream Come True

The American dream finally became a reality. No small credit can be given to the brave men and women who suffered. It is important that credit also be given to those of rank and stature who led and assisted the conflict.

> In Virginia an intolerant policy towards dissenters of all sorts was long maintained. Although the Episcopal ministers

were unpopular, the persons were few whose convictions led them to separate from the churches of the established faith, but the Baptists, Presbyterians and Quakers increased in numbers. As in Massachusetts, the approach of the Revolution led to a memorializing of the legislature of the colony in behalf of the separation of church and state, the petitioners expressing the hope that "in this enlightened age, and in a land where all of every denomination are united in the most strenuous efforts to be free," the legislature would agree to remove "every species of religious as well as civil bondage." Taking the position of Roger Williams, they affirmed that governments should be restricted to civil functions, that religion was a personal affair and one's duty to his God could only "be directed by reason and conviction." Remonstrances came from the other side, pointing out the value and prestige of the Establishment, and the colonial assembly spent a long time discussing the matter. The immediate result was the exemption of dissenters from ecclesiastical taxes, and the repeal of all laws enforcing attendance at the parish churches. Religious freedom became complete in 1785, when Thomas Jefferson championed the cause of religious equality, declaring that any restriction upon perfect religious liberty was infringement upon a natural right.[18]

Intolerance lasted longer in New England. Not until 1833 were the oppressive laws of Massachusetts removed from the record.

With the attainment of civil liberty came a spirit that made men see in religious persecution the tyranny and shame that it was. Virginia led the way, as became the colony that first made persecuting laws, and had equaled all others in the bitterness of her intolerance, if indeed she had not surpassed all. In 1629 the Assembly forbade any minister lacking Episcopal ordination to officiate in the colony, and this rule was enforced by severe penalties up to the Revolution. Baptists were also taxed for the support of the Episcopal Church and their property was seized and sold to pay such taxes. At length, however, they found champions in such men as Thomas Jefferson and Patrick Henry; the latter, though a member of the Established Church, being too genuine a lover of liberty to have any part in persecution. The first patriot legislature, which met in 1776, repealed the penal laws, and taxes for the support of the clergy were repealed in 1779. It was not until January, 1786, that the legislature passed an "Act for establishing religious freedom," drawn by Jefferson and powerfully advocated by James Madison.[19]

The American dream had been established: a wall of separation between the state and church. This great doctrine was implemented by conflict. Those who stood for God's way were a patriotic lot. When the Revolution came, they were among the first to stand. These Separatists had a great deal to gain. They fought for freedom of land and freedom of conscience. Their dream was that religious matters would no longer be governed by civil law.

What follows is of little worth if we miss this lesson of history. Everything we face in the current conflict must be candled in the light of what these people were trying to accomplish. When we ask, "What is the separation of church and state?" or determine what area it covers, we need only look at the record of those who suffered pain and death in the conflict. What did they struggle to destroy and build?

Footnotes

1. Dowley, p. 434.
2. Robert C. Newman, *Baptists and the American Tradition* (Schaumburg, IL: Regular Baptist Press, 1976), pp. 5, 6.
3. Ibid., pp. 6, 7.
4. Ibid., p. 3.
5. Albert Henry Newman, p. 287.
6. Norman E. Nygaard, *Champion of Liberty* (Grand Rapids: Zondervan Publishing House, 1964), pp. 47, 48.
7. Ibid., p. 49.
8. Ibid., p. 51.
9. Ibid., p. 70.
10. John Garrett, *Roger Williams: Witness Beyond Christendom—1603-1683* (London: Collier-Macmillan Ltd., 1970), p. 1.
11. Dowley, p. 483.
12. Garrett, p. 211.
13. Ibid., pp. 238, 239.
14. Robert Newman, p. 40.
15. Mecklin, p. 235.
16. Ibid., pp. 258, 259.
17. T. J. Villers, *Fidelity to Our Baptist Heritage,* ed. by R. T. Ketcham (Schaumburg, IL: General Association of Regular Baptist Churches, n.d.), p. 8.

18. Henry Kalloch Rowe, *The History of Religion of the United States* (New York: The Macmillan Co., 1928), pp. 50, 51.
19. Vedder, pp. 319, 320.

FIVE

The First Amendment and the Law

"Congress shall make no law respecting an establishment of religion, or prohibiting the free exercise thereof . . ." (U.S. Constitution).

WHAT IS SAID in this chapter may sound extremely radical if not taken fully in view of chapter 2 on Biblical authority. In spiritual matters the Bible, not the law, is supreme. For ecclesiastical direction God is the final authority, not the state.

An Example

Historically, this was the problem the state church faced with the Anabaptists. The issue of rebaptism was an affront to established power. In Dr. Ernest Pickering's excellent work, *Biblical Separation: The Struggle for a Pure Church,* he states:

> It was seen as subversive of the entire societal and ecclesiastical structure of the day, which viewed the church and the state as inextricably interwoven and interdependent. Thus, those who dared to rebaptize were thought of as seditious and worthy of the harshest punishment. They were challenging the divinely established order of things. They were separatists, made so by the very

> fact that they rejected the church-state concept and thus could not fellowship within its framework. . . .[1]

He continues to relate an incident that has contemporary meaning. Reformer and leader Ulrich Zwingli had a conflict with the Zurich town council. Since they were the civil-religious authorities, he told them he planned to conduct the Lord's table in a Bible manner. They opposed him and he did not press the issue, admitting one of two things: He either felt they were in power over the church or he was afraid. There were some who were not afraid; nor did they suppose that the civil government was over God.

> Such young men as Conrad Grebel (1495-1526) and Felix Manz (c. 1498-1527) felt that if the Scriptures taught something, it should be obeyed—regardless of what the city council thought. They remonstrated with Zwingli, but to no avail. Since they felt Zwingli lacked the courage of his convictions, they began to break with him.[2]

A Separatist View

The view that Biblical separatists must take is common to those who have suffered and died. There is no other God but the Lord. This was the view of those true believers who ushered in our constitutional government. That conviction was understood by great political leaders of the day who assisted in the framing of the law of the United States.

> In 1772, a general committee of Baptists was appointed to secure for all the colonies what was being so nobly won in Virginia. When the first Continental Congress convened at Philadelphia in 1774, this committee with Isaac Backus as leader presented a memorial pleading for "the inalienable rights of conscience to all." They were told by John Adams that so far as Massachusetts was concerned they might as well expect the planets to turn from their annual and diurnal course as to expect the Bay Colony to change its ecclesiastical establishment. But that Baptist committee believed in the perseverance of the saints. They persisted. They collected facts; they circulated petitions; they memorialized colonial assemblies until the national Constitution was adopted in 1787. Article VI provided that no religious test should ever be required as a qualification to any office or public trust under the United States. They saw that it would not prevent the government from erecting a state church. They consulted with Madison as to the wisest course of action;

> and on his advice they wrote directly to President Washington. In his reply he praised the Baptists as "the persevering promoters of our glorious revolution," and pledged himself to use all his influence in establishing effectual barriers against the horrors of spiritual tyranny and every species of religious persecution. One month after this correspondence, Madison, with the approval of Washington and in the language proposed by a committee of Virginia Baptists, introduced in the House of Representatives the First Amendment: "Congress shall make no law respecting an establishment of religion or prohibiting the free exercise thereof"; the most important writing since the canon of Scripture was closed and sealed with the stamp of Deity. On September 23, 1789, Congress adopted the amendment; and by December 15, 1791, it had been ratified by all the states except Massachusetts, Connecticut, and Georgia. And so at last, after generations of suffering, the Baptist idea had become the American idea. At last, after centuries of bloodshed, the despised old Baptist doctrine of soul liberty had become a part of our national law; and America in the widest sense was the land of the free as well as the home of the brave. Such is our glorious heritage of soul liberty, a heritage which we are bound to defend and extend and bequeath.[3]

The establishment of constitutional law was, in reality, a fulfillment of the pilgrim dream. It was their reason for coming to the New World.

> The motives provoking men and women to brave the risks of a sea voyage, and risk their lives and fortunes in a strange and hostile continent, were shared quite generally by this brave and hearty group. There was a desire to get away from the endless wars and conflicts in Europe; there was resolve to get away from the snatching and selling of men for service in the armies and navies of kings and princes who were forever at war; there was a longing to find honest and honorable work and to create better homes for themselves and their children; and there was an eagerness to escape religious persecutions and to found communities where they could worship God in their own ways.[4]

Constitution Ratification

So much suffering could not be ignored in setting the guidelines for this new nation. When the Constitution was taken to the states for ratification, however, there was a common reaction from the people. We need to make an issue of those attitudes which brought about the Bill of Rights.

> When the Constitution was taken to the various state ratifying conventions it soon became evident that the folks back home felt that the document did not go far enough, that a mere inference to be drawn from its one mention of religion was not sufficient. They felt they could trust themselves to do the right thing about both individual and institutional religion, but they could not trust their neighbors. Lest a combination of their neighbors in the new Federal Government foist on them principles or practices they abhorred, they clamored for a Federal Bill of Rights.[5]

It is important to note that this was no small reaction. Our present conflict can be settled by an understanding of what transpired. No less than five states suggested a bill of rights with their ratification. New Hampshire, New York and Virginia all pressed for a clear declaration of religious freedom. The first Congress, therefore, was faced with a variety of suggestions. There was still a diversity of religious views. In the states where freedom had not been won, such as Virginia, there could have been adverse reaction. Feeling in favor of the Bill of Rights ran high, as illustrated here.

> Following its completion, the Constitution (without a Bill of Rights) was submitted to the state legislatures for ratification. Strong opposition to the Constitution arose. Patrick Henry, a Christian, declared, "I look upon that paper as the most fatal plan that could possibly be conceived to enslave a free people." A significant faction of men such as Patrick Henry, George Mason, and Richard Henry Lee moved to stop ratification if the Constitution was not amended to include a Bill of Rights. In fact, Patrick Henry's long and excellent oratories on the subject were a prime factor in the emergence of the first ten amendments to the Constitution.[6]

When the amendment on religion was first proposed to the full house it read:

> "No religion shall be established by law, nor shall the equal rights of conscience be infringed." After some debate the House changed the Committee's proposed amendment to read: "that Congress shall make no laws touching religion, or infringing the rights of conscience."[7]

John W. Whitehead in *The Separation Illusion* makes a very interesting observation about this event.

> The Constitution was devoid of a Bill of Rights when it

> emerged from the Philadelphia Convention in 1787. This omission was the basis of the most crucial and serious criticisms of the new Constitution by the state conventions (although they finally ratified it). It was felt that a Bill of Rights "would protect fundamental rights against interference by the new federal government." This fear of Big Brother eventually produced the Bill of Rights as the first ten amendments to the Constitution in 1791.[8]

To understand the meaning of the First Amendment we need to know what the people and the framers meant.

> The absolute guarantees of the First Amendment reflected the keen awareness of the people of the experiences with religious persecution and bigotry suffered by the early colonists, and "of conditions and practices which they fervently wished to stamp out in order to preserve liberty for themselves and for their posterity." The basic premise of the amendment was rooted in the deep belief that the legitimate areas of influence of church and state can best be served if each is "free from the other within its respective sphere." There was also the desire in the minds of the people that no one denomination or any combination of denominations would ever become strong enough to exercise undue influence on the state or on persons of conflicting opinions and beliefs.[9]

A Bill of Rights

It is incredible that a student of history could view the total setting as described herein and not understand what it means. The Constitution was, without the Bill of Rights, not acceptable. It may have solved the oppressive actions of government, as they felt them from mother England, but it did not solve the religious oppression they had felt in the new land. What would keep Congress from making laws that said a church, its ministries and ministers had to be licensed and approved? How would the Constitution, without a Bill of Rights, keep the future state and her agencies from demanding control over materials taught in the church?

The protestors were dissenters from the previous fraud practiced upon the true church. They would not pay taxes to support a state church; nor would they be compelled, by law, to believe or practice other creeds. The answer to the Constitution as it stood was *no.* In fact, it became a very unpopular document. The concept of a state church, a church state or the civil control of the church was out of the question. This was not just the view of churchmen.

> What is perhaps more important, the proponents of liberty, whether or not they were known primarily as churchmen, whether or not they were strong defenders of the faith, came more and more to recognize the religious aspect of freedom in general. Religious faith was seen as the sanction of liberty, and religious liberty, freedom of conscience, as the fountainhead of all the other liberties.[10]

This spirit can be felt in the acts passed in the Virginia Assembly in 1786.

> Be it therefore enacted by the General Assembly, that no man shall be compelled to frequent or support any religious worship, place or ministry whatsoever, nor shall be enforced, restrained, molested, or burthened in his body or goods, nor shall otherwise suffer on account of his religious opinions or belief; but that all men shall be free to profess, and by argument to maintain, their opinions in matters of religion, and that the same shall in nowise diminish, enlarge, or affect their civil capacities.[11]

Consider those who were not true believers or solid supporters of the religious freedom concept. Their reaction was one of cooperation, by reason that they could accomplish their goals politically and so:

> Madison, one of the leaders of the First Congress, although strongly in favor of a bill of rights, considered specific prohibitions not "essential" but had no objection to them since they were neither "improper nor altogether useless" and were "anxiously desired by others." In deference to the fears and demands of several of the ratifying states, Madison presented to Congress an amendment which he thought incorporated the desires of these states: . . .[12]

The result of this tidal wave of religious concern and cooperation was the First Amendment: "Congress shall make no law respecting an establishment of religion, or prohibiting the free exercise thereof." So brief but so all-encompassing. Unbelievable as it was, the establishment of religious freedom became a reality.

> This view of church and state is so ingrained in the American consciousness that it requires some effort to imagine what a radical concept and daring innovation it was when our Constitution was being framed. For more than fourteen hundred years it had been assumed, virtually universally, that the stability of

> the social and political order depends on the religious solidarity of the people. No ruler or statesman, no religious or social philosopher, no church official or other responsible thinker had dared to question this axiom until our founding fathers observed settling in this land peoples of different and often antagonistic religious orientations. Our founders were intelligent, practical men who came to see an experiment with religious pluralism as virtually unavoidable; if the states were to be united, there must be national religious freedom.[13]

Important to our understanding of this establishment in America is the response of new states. Those that were later admitted to the union came with an affirmation of religious freedom and the division of church and state.

> The constitution of Kentucky of 1792, for example, provided that "no preference shall ever be given by law to any religious societies or modes of worship" and that "the civil rights, privileges or capacities of any citizens shall in no ways be diminished or enlarged on account of his religion." The constitution of Minnesota (1857) provided: ". . . nor shall any control of or interference with the rights of conscience be permitted, or any preference be given by law to any religious establishment or mode of worship. . . ." Many of the provisions of the constitutions of several states regarding religion are borrowed from one another. Alabama's constitution (1867, revised 1875 and 1901 but retaining the same article) says curtly: "No person shall be deprived of the right to worship God according to the dictates of his own conscience." The Bill of Rights of the constitution of New Mexico (1912), the 47th state to be admitted to the Union, uses the same language in more extended form:
>
>> Every man shall be free to worship God according to the dictates of his own conscience, and no person shall ever be molested or denied any civil or political right or privilege on account of his religious opinion or mode of religious worship. No person shall be required to attend any place of worship or support any religious sect or denomination; nor shall any preference be given by law to any religious denomination or mode of worship.[14]

What Did It Mean?

There does not seem to be any question in the actions of those who stood by at the birth of our nation. They knew what they meant.

But we live in a day of conflict. We shall discuss later the established state church of the nineteenth century. While there is an unwarranted fear of a coming church state (that is both improbable and unacceptable), there is grave danger to the church. Her separatist position is all but lost, and religious freedom will soon only be words. The reason is that we have allowed pseudo-authorities to answer the question, "What does the First Amendment mean?"

This particular problem speaks to the heart of the issue. The issues facing the courts today deal with the limitation of civil power over the church. No amount of semantics or debate can change what has been established as the purpose of the First Amendment. Every statement we make must be viewed with that historical perspective. Let us look at the words of the First Amendment.

Congress. This is a satisfactory reference to civil power. The dissident's problem was not with a particular governor or assembly. This entry into the Bill of Rights affects all levels of temporal power, including those bureaucracies and agencies responsible to them.

No law. This is a reflection on the multitude of rules, regulations, standards and statutes meant to hinder the freedom of the soul and control of the church. When the leaders responded to the cry of those ratifying states, they meant no law of any kind at any level would be acceptable. In our other discourses we challenge the validity of any such civil law and ask, "Is a law in violation of the First Amendment regardless of what a court rules a law?" That needs to be reconsidered in light of the serious violations of government.

There are two things in the amendment that the civil authorities are not allowed to do: (1) establish a religion; (2) prohibit the free exercise thereof. Current interpretations have tried, either out of ignorance or deliberate pretense, to cloud the meaning of this statement. The simple truth is that the knowledgeable, informed writers of the Bill of Rights knew exactly what they were doing. Whatever is not covered in the first statement is carefully covered in the second. No action of church or state ought to be commenced unless it clears with historical meaning of both these precepts. At present, the legislatures and courts are respecting only the first part of this amendment.

Opponents may wish to dismiss all this as the rambling of a theologian. I am not an attorney and do not intend to present these maxims as legal advice. It would be an absolute waste of creativity to enter into legal argument from that point of view. I speak as a dissident. These words are the words of those who paid dearly to give this nation the only example of religious freedom. I speak as one who is willing to pay a great price to keep what is being forcibly removed from us. The state has found that not all churches are asleep and would rather fight than switch. Death is sweeter than oppressive government bitterness, if that means forsaking the eternal authority of God.

Let us go back to the acceptance of the Bill of Rights as added in 1791.

> The path toward the enactment of this Amendment had been a long and tortuous one, and it is probably because of this long and arid journey that the "meat" of the Amendment is so succinctly stated, so admirably "laid on the line." Since its enactment, both State and Church have worked—each in its own sphere and way, and with extraordinary success—for the welfare of mankind. By keeping, each to its own bailiwick, peace has been established and kept between the two institutions, and the Scriptural distinction between Church and State has been manifest on a national scale.
>
> The First Amendment to our Constitution provides a *legal* separation between Church and State: *not a moral nor a spiritual* separation. It provides simply, that Congress cannot establish a denomination as the favored religion nor can it prohibit any denomination from establishing itself on American soil. *The wall of separation is legal, we repeat, not moral or spiritual.* There is no reason, under the Constitution of the United States, why the principles of Christianity cannot pervade the laws and institutions of the United States of America.[15]

Spiritual Authority

There is no quarrel that the enactment of the amendment was a legal act. From the very first until recent years it has worked with very little conflict. The current violation by civil authorities leads us to view the statement by J. Marcellus Kik: The separation stands because of the spiritual authority that stands behind it. Therefore, the issue is primarily Biblical with only the recognition of law supporting it. When the Constitution is recognized from this point of view, it does not allow for the moral influence of society. It further recognized that our founding fathers saw the validity of Biblical morals and government principles. One would be something less than honest not to recognize their inclusion as part of our original laws.

Civil authorities have not yet recognized the folly of attempting to legislate morality, however.

> There is need, moreover, that the churches re-examine their doctrine of morality. We no longer put our trust in princes, but we are strangely dependent upon legislation. There is need for discrimination between legislation designed to prevent injustice and legislation designed to make men just. It seems absurd that, after centuries of experience, we should have to remind ourselves that morality cannot be induced by law.[16]

The power of the church is to affect and influence change on the world. Those areas that God has given to the church are to be carried out by the church law, not civil law.

> It is in this light that we must view our obligation to promote political change for the sake of the poor and oppressed. If the greed and covetousness of a rich man were being manifested in such a way that no one but him was being oppressed by his activities, we would not have the right to attempt to change his behavior by coercion. We should preach to him, even plead with him to forsake his self-destructive ways, but we ought not try to "legislate" his behavior.[17]

Just as the church is responsible for its charge, so is the state. It operates only under the permission and authority of the sovereign God. While it is true that the state must make laws to punish the murderer, that is done under God's command. It is not the prerogative of civil authorities to require church attendance and other spiritual matters.

The Right Words

It is argued that the First Amendment does not include the words *church* or *state*. That is of no consequence. We know what the writers meant because we know why the people required its addition. The concept is this: *Congress* meant the civil power that had plagued the separatists. It meant all state power. The church, for the dissident, included all levels of spiritual exercise.

The problem of dealing with legal philosophers is that they never stand still. Nothing is ever a fact to them. Static truth is elusive.

> American theories of religious freedom, all of them, have one legal starting point when they are put into practice—the two religion clauses of the First Amendment to the federal Constitution. The relationship of the First Amendment to the law of the fifty states will be discussed later. The clauses' words

> are few—just sixteen. "Congress shall make no law respecting an establishment of religion, or prohibiting the free exercise thereof." Nowhere does the Constitution define these terms. They were not borrowed from well-developed British law on the subject. Since in 1791 when this amendment was ratified and today when we continue to use it, people differ on the legal meaning of "religion" and "establishment" and "free exercise," we must recognize that our constitutional starting point for freedom of religion is general or ambiguous or vague.[18]

It is not ambiguous to those on the battle line. There is nothing theoretical about the threat of imprisonment. Only maniacs die for suppositions. Patriots die for the truth they have lived for. We know the meaning of *no law* of establishment or prohibition because we know the truth the instigators of this amendment lived.

A second argument is given that there is no legal statement erecting a "wall of separation" between church and state. One would agree or disagree based on what is being done with the wall.

> In 1962 and 1963 with two momentous decisions the Supreme Court declared death to God in the public schools of this country. Nietzche's nightmarish death wish seemed a reality, and God somehow had become unconstitutional.
>
> The Court ruled that the so-called wall of separation which supposedly stood between church and state, prevented the use of state-directed prayer and Bible reading in the public schools. This utilization of government-directed prayer, the Court declared, was a violation of the establishment-of-religion clause in the First Amendment of the Constitution.
>
> Hugo Black, author of the school-prayer decision, gave the classic interpretation of the First Amendment establishment clause. In a 1947 decision Justice Black said, "In the words of Jefferson, the clause against establishment of religion by law was intended to erect a 'wall of separation between church and state.' "[19]

The fact that those words do not appear or that a supposed wall is moved around to please the church or state is not the issue. A line of demarcation, a gulf, a wall of separation does exist by God's rule as shown in chapter 1. On one side He placed certain responsibilities; on the other, a second set. Only a heavenly authoritative voice can make such statements, and the voices of His prophets need to thunder that truth in this day of coming persecution.

The phrases "separation of church and state" and "religious freedom" have been used freely in these chapters. Do they mean the same thing? The beauty of the First Amendment is that it recognizes God's law from two points of view. The separation principle does not include all religious freedom as it applies to the church. Religious freedom does include the church-state division, however. What God-guided wisdom there was in the omission of the former is in the enactment of the amendment in question.

Is Freedom Just a Statement?

I will persist that the separation of church and state as the present rulers interpret it is meant to separate the church from the state at every level. However, they practice the attachment of the state to the church at any level. An excellent example of this is the matter of taxation that is being pressed upon the church by a hypercritical society of legalists. At this point, it means nothing to these apostles of theory that the law forbids them to interfere with the church.

> The Soviet Union has, in its constitution, an impressive guarantee of the freedom of religion. This "guarantee" is, of course, worthless, because other laws make this "right" totally subject to state permits, regulations and controls. As a consequence, the constitutional guarantee is worthless.[20]

Without our understanding, but with our apathetic consent, government has begun to make our religious freedom null and void. The process is simple; just add laws, taxes and standards from dictatorial bureaucracies to erase the power of freedom of religion. Alexander de Chalandeau, a veteran of Iron Curtain travel, explains this procedure in *The Christians in the U.S.S.R.*

> When V. I. Lenin came into power, he promised full liberty of worship to all Soviet citizens, and laws were passed granting this privilege. Today these laws have not changed, but in practice they have not been applied since 1928.
>
> 1. **The Soviet Laws.** It was on January 23, 1918, after the Soviet Revolution, that a decree was adopted in the USSR and the following laws were passed dealing with the separation of church and state. The translation of these laws was taken from the US Senate.[21]

What follows is a list of restrictions that makes many pronouncements of religious liberty. It is to control where the church meets and where the church serves. The Russian laws are zoning, health, welfare, education, licensing and safety. Under the guise that the state knows best, personal and church religious liberties are lost.

Even in the darkness of a powerful communistic society, a pretense is made to show that freedom exists. Approved groups may remain active under the constant eye of the KGB. Every oppressive state will always find weaklings who will compromise anything to protect their own. Many in America have been fooled into believing that Russian Christians have some form of religious freedom. What is happening in the United States is the same story.

Are we hinting that the United States civil authorities are violating the law in the destruction of guaranteed religious liberties? In reading the documented record of existing persecution in our land you can decide for yourself.

Those in government power are not the only violators of this freedom. Large church groups and denominations, including the Roman Catholic Church, encourage such destruction. They would agree that the state is not to favor one religion over another. They believe, however, that the government could support religion equally. Support of church ministries such as schools could be subsidized equally they say. The result is that they take all they can get from the state. That surely is the reason they do not dare see or speak out on the destruction of religious liberty in the United States.

We need to settle it in our minds once and for all. It is wrong to take anything from the state, for what is theirs to give they will control. The government, state or federal, cannot aid one religion in deference to another. Neither can it aid all on an equal basis.

> In paraphrasing Justice Black above, I deliberately left out two passages. The first of these said that under the establishment clause, government could not aid all religions equally. The justice is legally correct on this point. The Court has said so over and over again.[22]

Difficult Reevaluation

We need to seriously rethink all of these areas. A gradual change in our attitude has brought some dangerous compromises. The state can carry out its God-ordained functions without violating the church. The church, on the other hand, must maintain her Biblical responsibilities without being sustained by the state.

> Yes, in the State as in the Church and in the family, the will of God is supreme. But the State, the family, the Church, are different institutions, existing for different ends, and securing

> their ends by different methods. In each there is Authority, but in each the Authority is of a different kind, possesses different powers, and asserts those powers by different instruments. We want the will of God to be done in the State; we want the laws of the State and the policy of the State to be in harmony with the will of God; but what is the will of God in relation to the State?
>
> It is our belief that the Church and the State, though both of them are Divine institutions, are Divine institutions of such a different description, and with such different immediate objects, that any organic alliance between them is certain in the long run to be injurious to both.[23]

This careful line of reconsideration will be traumatic. The church must realize that the acceptance of favors from the civil government opened the door to control, particularly in education. Where the government pays, it rules. The other side of this radical dissection is the government's responsibility to cease all control, penalty and taxation of any church ministry.

One of the reasons the church has lost its direction, vitality and purity is due to the compromise. She has sold herself to the state like a woman of the street. A welfare mentality has gripped our people. Leadership must rise to deny the state any further encroachment. She must repent of her illicit involvement.

> The church, on the other hand, standing for the individual, cannot tolerate any inroad upon the *inner* life of her people. If any legislature, or executive officer, or even any high court of justice, should attempt to regulate the belief or thought of the people, she, as a body of people acting in their capacity as individuals, would once more become a church of Covenanters, Nonjurors, resisting by sacrifice. She knows there is an inward zone of morality in the heart of the individual where compromise is naked guilt. To maintain the purity of that zone she will, if need be, go out to the cross—with perfect faith in her resurrection on the third day.[24]

The coming of compromise and the spoiling of the church is not a recent happening. This problem has been in the making as early as 1910.

> Great changes have taken place since 1910 in actual relationships between church and state in many countries of the world, and also in thought and attitudes on such relationships. The state has changed much, the church somewhat. States of modern type have greatly extended their function, dominating

large fields of human activity and dwarfing church efforts in education, medicine, and other services. Masses of citizens have come to feel that only the state has the material resources and the numerous technicians required for adequate meeting of human needs—apart from a narrow strip designated as spiritual or religious. In the minds of many, not merely the church but even God himself is displaced by the state, which appears to be the providence of daily bread, of healing, of moral standards, of hope for a better ordering of community life.[25]

Cry of the Concerned

We dare go no farther. Everyone who is sensitive to the American dream will need to speak out. This is not a time for philosophy. It is a time to return to our established law, for everyone to obey it. We know what our forefathers meant; it did work and it will work. In 1844 William Jones Seaburg wrote:

> "The Church and the State are distinct communities, the governments have jurisdiction partly concurrent and partly complementary: concurrent in so far as they extend over the same territory and relate to the same persons; complementary in respect to their administration of law. . . ."[26]

What will happen if civil government continues to push her state church, her present religion of humanism? We will return to pre-Constitution days. Control of religion by those who are not able to control themselves is already upon us. There will always be the compromisers. There will also be the true patriots, the nonconformists. Will they pick up arms and fight a lawless state? No, they will repeat the story of the Anabaptists, Roger Williams and the dissenters of Virginia. This discourse is meant to be a warning. The state is asking us to license our church ministries. We will not do that! We cannot do that and be true to God and the Bible. Next, the state will tell us to close our ministries and it will confiscate our buildings. History tells us this will not work, but only suffering can follow the coming conflict.

Absurd you say! Well, read the documented record that follows. We are already in the conflict. The position of godly people must be: "Civil authorities will make *no* law establishing or prohibiting freedom of religion."

Footnotes

1. Ernest Pickering, *Biblical Separation: The Struggle for a Pure Church* (Schaumburg, IL: Regular Baptist Press, 1979), pp. 43, 44.
2. Ibid., pp. 44, 45.
3. Villers, p. 9.
4. "Precepts of Our Pilgrim Heritage," address of Lt. General James V. Edmundson, U.S. Air Force (Ret.) to the Florida State Meeting of the Order of Founders and Patriots, January 20, 1979, in *News & Views,* (November 1979).
5. Merrimon Cuninggim, *Freedom's Holy Light* (New York: Harper & Brothers, 1955), p. 96.
6. John W. Whitehead, *The Separation Illusion* (Milford, MI: Mott Media, 1977), p. 41.
7. Albert C. Huegli, ed., *Church and State under God* (St. Louis: Concordia Publishing House, 1964), pp. 261.
8. Whitehead, p. 65.
9. Huegli, p. 262.
10. Cuninggim, p. 36.
11. Verna Hall, comp., Joseph Allan Montgomery, ed., *Self-Government with Union: Christian History of the Constitution Series,* Vol. II (San Francisco: The American Christian Constitution Press, 1962), p. 60.
12. Huegli, p. 261.
13. Perry C. Cotham, *Politics, Americanism and Christianity* (Grand Rapids: Baker Book House, 1976), p. 132.
14. Huegli, p. 205.
15. J. Marcellus Kik, *Church and State* (New York: Thomas Nelson & Sons, 1963), p. 116.
16. Umphrey Lee, *Render unto the People* (New York: Abingdon-Cokesbury Press, 1947), p. 137.
17. Richard J. Mouw, *Politics and the Biblical Drama* (Grand Rapids: Wm. B. Eerdmans Publishing Co., 1976), p. 80. Used by permission.
18. Walfred H. Peterson, *Thy Liberty in Law* (Nashville: Convention Press, 1978), pp. 39, 40. Used by permission.
19. Whitehead, p. 88.
20. R. J. Rushdoony, "Is Separation of Church and State Really Religious Freedom?" *Cornerstone,* (June 1979), p. 1.
21. Alexander de Chalandeau, *The Christians in the U.S.S.R.* (Chicago: Harper and Co., 1978), p. 121.
22. Peterson, p. 152.
23. R. W. Dale, *Fellowship with Christ* (London: Hodder & Stoughton, 1907), pp. 203, 204.
24. Lynn Harold Hough, *Whither Christianity?* (New York: Harper

& Brothers, 1929), pp. 199, 200.

25. Lefferts A. Loetscher, ed., *Twentieth Century Encyclopedia of Religious Knowledge,* Vol. I (Grand Rapids: Baker Book House, 1955), p. 247.

26. Hall, p. 64.

SIX

Education, the Catalyst

"The fundamental theory of liberty upon which all governments in this Union repose excludes any general power of the State to standardize its children by forcing them to accept instruction from public education only. The child is not the creature of the State; those who nurture him and direct his destiny have the right, as well as the high duty, to recognize and prepare him for additional duties" (U.S. Supreme Court).

THAT EDUCATION is the business of the church is evidenced in chapter 1. For the Christian, education is not acceptable outside a spiritual environment. There are no secular areas in a Christian's life. No subject is without the area of spiritual influence. Bible integration is a must to balance knowledge and wisdom (1 Cor. 10:31).

Education for children in the state-federal system no longer has any resemblance to wisdom. Academic tragedy, like a plague, has passed throughout our land. The fruit of incompetence is everywhere. The statists hurry to cover the shame of their nakedness. As a people who have expelled God, they have injured pride.

The second tragedy we discussed centers around the fact that the government, by bureaucratic power, demands that the church school follow their record of failure. The lie was so thorough that a takeover of all education was almost accomplished. In the nick of time God moved upon our hearts. The great Christian school growth has posed a major threat to the power grab. If the church would have been as deeply immersed in state control as its ministry of education, it would have never recovered.

Education in Conflict

Education in conflict has been the catalyst for a return to religious freedom. Without our knowledge, or consent, the same things that have gripped the church's ministry of education would have crushed the church. It is not too late if godly Biblicists will heed the warnings.

The battle is presently being fought in a specific ministry of the church: the church school. I concede that I do not see the state-federal school as savable. To accomplish that we would have to go back through time, step by step, until we came to the church schools which were the first educational units that existed in our country.

In review, I see the role of education as belonging to the church. There is no Biblical precedent for the state to educate. Since, therefore, the state's role in education of the children of the church is unwise, it is also a violation of the separation of church and state. This explains, in part, the state's inability to succeed in educating the total man. The state will claim victory, citing the literacy rate in the United States. That record was established before the state school came into existence and before God was expelled. The state's record is now echoed in the words, "Johnny still can't read."

Educators must face the fact that the return to church schools is a reality. We must assess the results. The state and the education unions have so much at issue that they are not taking this challenge without action. Until now these powers have been using bureaucratic officials to harass the church. First this was done through threats and paper abuse. Now churches are being hauled into court by the dozens. What is their crime? Obeying the Word of God in training their own children. What has happened to America when the civil authorities again punish Christians for spiritual activities? In the words of Patrick Henry, "Great God!"

One must be keenly aware that Christians by the thousands do not know the score or the time. That is the purpose of these pages. However, these sincere friends try to revive a rotting corpse through Bible reading, Bible study and prayer in the state schools. An individual might be helped in some small way, but is this the answer? Let me ask you for another radical consideration. If it is true that the federal educational system does belong to the government, is it not wrong, before God, to violate the separation of church and state and involve religion?

> We think that the constitutional prohibition against laws respecting an establishment of religion must at least mean that in this country it is no part of the business of government to compose official prayers for any group of the American people to recite as part of a religious program carried on by government.[1]

If these dear people really believe that God belongs in education, why not do it without violation—in the church school? The state schools have rightly been termed the "Philistine schools." They are not, in fact, in action or purpose, Christian. Almost everything about them is opposed to a God-directed philosophy of Christian education.

In the *Detroit Free Press* an article appeared with a headline telling the story: "Church and State in a Life-and-Death Education Battle."[2] At issue are the church schools in North Carolina. This article openly recognizes the fact that there are two kinds of schools in this battle—church schools and state schools. The crime of these church schools is that they refuse to lower themselves to the standards of the state. The Christian schools have rightly refused to violate the separation of church and state by recognizing the Philistine schools as an authority. They will not report to them.

The State-Federal School

If you have enough fortitude and fairness, take a look at the dying state system. *U.S. News & World Report* of January 26, 1976, reported on vandalism and violence in an article entitled, "Terror in Schools."[3] School-related homicides increased by 18 percent, rapes by 40 percent, robberies by 37 percent, assault by 85 percent, assaults on teachers by 77 percent and related offenses 38 percent. With $600 million a year in vandalism, the greatest need remaining is discipline. So serious was the situation in Chicago that there were 70 security guards at the cost of $3 million. Also, $3.2 million had to be spent on equipment and programs for security and $3.5 million to cover property losses. A Gallup poll lists the ranking of problems.

1. Lack of discipline
2. Integration/segregation
3. Lack of proper financial support
4. Difficulty of getting good teachers

5. Use of drugs
6. Size of school/classes
7. Crime/vandalism/stealing
8. Poor curriculum and pupils' lack of interest
9. Parents' lack of interest and lack of proper facilities
10. School boards' policies[4]

These are the people who are going to tell God's people how to run God's school system? It has to be the extreme in hypocrisy. Can you imagine the rabbis of Israel going over to the Philistine school system and asking them to oversee the teachings of Israel's children? It would be almost as incredible as Israel sending her children to the Philistine camp for five days of education after her Sabbath school.

Listen to the current news: A boy's prom date plan perplexed school administrators. Why? He wanted to take a boy. I can tell you that would not be a consideration in a Biblical church school.

Several years ago in our small-town community it came to my attention that something similar was to transpire for commencement exercises at the local state school. The band was preparing to play an arrangement called, "Statement." It was during the Vietnam Conflict. The band was to shout at intervals such things as, "Make love, not babies"; "Honorable and just peace"; "Women's liberation"; "Brotherhood, not motherhood"; "Population is everybody's baby"; "Power to the people" and, "Hell, no, we won't go." I do not know how much my protest had to do with it, but it was not used.

Our protests have been too few and too infrequent. Now every weirdo is welcome as student or employee. Sodomites seduce our young people, booze is better; and they not only sit on the grass at school, they smoke it. There are no excuses that have not been used a dozen times to defend this ailing "King of Education." One would think that such a powerful educational monopoly could destroy its competition by simply doing a better job, particularly since it has absconded with all the education taxes for its own use.

The destruction is not going to be done through a better product because the state school has failed the course in academic excellence. Meanwhile, the Christian school passed with honors. The reason humanists must use illicit methods to destroy those who embarrass them with outstanding academics and discipline is not only that they expelled God, it is that they replaced the true sovereign God with the religion of humanism, and the god of humanism is man.

> Secular education has its faith and its values and these have a decided religious impact. The Supreme Court itself has said that the faith *that there is no Supreme Being* constitutes a

> religious conviction and is to be respected as such. Secular education affirms in faith that 'in the beginning was chance,' that man is an animal, that truth is relative, that history has no meaning, that life has no purpose and that death is the end. These are all articles of faith. Teaching of these articles of faith constitutes an establishment of religion. The use of tax money to support this significantly assails the constitutional rights of Bible believing citizens. The constitutional rights of a significant number of citizens are being significantly assailed.[5]

Uninformed

All of this may sound like a diatribe against secular education. In reality it is my desire to sound a *warning*. Those of us who have the smell of battle upon our clothes speak with a different voice, and we need to learn patience with those who are uninformed.

I was shocked some time ago when I wrote an official of the "Americans United for Separation of Church and State." Not only was there a lack of understanding about the concept of state schools, but no understanding or knowledge at all of the self-professed religion of humanism in that educational system. I quote the reply of this official, "As for Secular Humanism, we readily admit that there is a religious position called Secular Humanism. What we can find no evidence to support, however, is the idea that Secular Humanism is actually being promoted in the public schools by the teachers, administrators, and school board members who are a rough cross section of the religious spectrum of the community." I was reminded of the Russian cosmonaut who soared out into space and upon returning stated he had looked for God but was unable to see Him.

The church school is often criticized by the uninformed. They call it "Cadillac education," "a hothouse," "academically inferior" and "a luxury." Our statements about the state school are not meant to defame persons related to it. We intend to demonstrate practically, Biblically, morally and academically that the Philistine system has no power over the superior church school system. Furthermore, church schools are not a luxury, they are a necessity. Education by the state that includes God does appear to be a violation, an unholy collusion of church and state. On the other hand, education without Him, for the Christian, is forbidden by God (Prov. 1:7; Col. 3:17).

In the book *Education for the Real World,* Henry M. Morris uses a whole chapter to deal with "humanistic and superhumanistic education." Based on his explanation of secularized education, the Christian could only have one reaction.

In this chapter we wish to examine more closely the two systems, both built on the foundation and framework of evolution, that have dominated educational theory and practice in every non-Christian society of the past or present. These systems are humanism and what might be called "superhumanism." Other possible terms are naturalism and supernaturalism, rationalism and irrationalism, materialism and immaterialism. One system views man as the pinnacle of the evolutionary process and as the ultimate arbiter of meaning; the other considers the spirit world beyond the physical as a higher order of existence toward which all things evolve. The first system is man-centered, the second is ultimately Satan-centered. Modern man, having rejected Biblical theism, must turn either to naturalistic humanism or supernaturalistic occultism.[6]

Everything identified here with humanism is present in the state school system. We need to ask, "Why?" The answer is that man will always move to responses of the flesh when God is not an option. You cannot have a pure productive society or education without God. The following comparison demonstrates the difference in approach.

	Man-Centered	God-Centered
Materialism	1 Tim. 6:5-10	1 John 2:15-17
Intellectualism	2 Tim. 3:7	2 Cor. 10:5
Hedonism	Rom. 1:26, 27	Rom. 13:14
Spiritualism (occult)	1 Tim. 4:1-3	1 John 4:1
Evolution	Rom. 1:21-23	Col. 1:16
Satanism	Dan. 3:3-6	Acts 5:29
Rationalism	2 Tim. 3:8	John 17:17
Progressivism	1 Tim. 6:5	Heb. 13:8
Rights	Judges 21:25	Rom. 12:1-3
Reformation	2 Tim. 3:5	John 3:3
Uncertainty	Eccles. 11:9	2 Tim. 1:12

This obvious division of direction leads us to a sobering conclusion. The church could not be controlled by a system so vastly different. In holistic education, civil authorities would be incompetent. This is the major issue. Who will control the church schools? The conflict, then, brings a repeated conclusion to the surface. The church must not be controlled organizationally by federal education.

That is a violation of separation. Viewing the First Amendment as we have, we must decline civil control over a church school at any level.

An Old Problem

There is some disagreement about church education from the beginning of the church. William Barclay says the church did not have schools because of their strong view on the imminence of the Second Coming, their poverty and:

> Still further, it was not so very long before Christianity became illegal. When the time came when a man could be regarded as a criminal simply for the name of Christian, and not because of any crimes attaching to the name, Christian schools would be an obvious impossibility. No body of people who were automatically outside the law could possibly set up their own schools.[7]

No one would quarrel with those considerations. But the home was the center of activity and education in those days of persecution. The New Testament demonstrates in the Great Commission that the church's role in education was consistent and preeminent. There were times when persecution was not in evidence and then:

> "The Christians took all possible care to accustom their children to the study of the scriptures, and to instruct them in the doctrines of their holy religion; and schools were every where erected for this purpose, even from the very commencement of the Christian church. . . ."[8]

Godly Teachers

The church's claim from the beginning has been to train her own. The writer of Proverbs warns about training by those who are not godly: "Cease, my son, to hear the instruction that causeth to err from the words of knowledge" (Prov. 19:27). The teacher is so important that Luke 6:40 records: "A pupil is not above his teacher; but everyone, after he has been fully trained, will be like his teacher" (NASB). Teachers pass life-styles and philosophy to students, so Paul wrote, "Beware lest any man spoil you through philosophy and vain deceit, after the tradition of men, after the rudiments of the world, and not after Christ" (Col. 2:8).

During the reign of Julian there was not only a deliberate monoply of education but a control of teachers.

> And now the aim of Julian was quite clear, it was to close the secular schools against all Christian teachers. They must either abandon their belief in Christianity, and return to belief in the old pagan gods, or cease to teach.[9]

The struggle to control education still rages through the educators. The plan for licensing teachers is so promulgated as to deliberately discriminate against godly teachers who, in many cases, are far superior to certified ones. But the name of the conflict is not superior education, as the state has confessed. It is control. In the aforementioned book by Henry M. Morris there is a chapter on "The Teaching and the Teacher." Under qualifications of teachers he lists:

1. Spiritual Qualifications
2. Professional Qualifications
3. Biblical Maturity
4. Experience and Wisdom[10]

I wonder if the state would like to have to include these for certification. First, it would eradicate most of its personnel. Second, it would cry, "Violation of the separation of church and state." Exactly, but these are the qualifications of the church school teacher. To require things of those that are opposed to the philosophy of Christian education is hypocritical. We cry, "Violation of separation."

This section began with a consideration that the school issue brought conflict into the open. The control of teachers is paramount. In time the state violators could have closed the door on Christian educators. Now they must face the issue. What do you do with Christian teachers who will not seek the approval of unqualified humanists? You destroy them lawlessly. You make laws against God and punish the best educators with incarceration.

God-centered Education

Another area in the conflict over education is curriculum. If the statists are allowed to control curriculum in violation to the separation principle, what would happen? Obviously the requirements would be humanistic. Each of these subjects will be dealt with under licensing, but can the state determine what will be taught in any ministry of the church? This has progressed farther than you would imagine. In the *Argus-Press,* Owosso, Michigan, May 3, 1978, the headline reads, "Can Court Decide What Church Should Teach?" The court did decide what the church should teach, and it is used throughout the schools in violation of the First Amendment. In Utah the court refused to allow credit for Bible courses. That was in a state school. What about the church school?

The vain imagination of secular educators is that there is a division between secular and religious education. For the believer this is impossible. Everything is sacred to him (1 Cor. 10:31). The limited mind views this teaching as "nonacademic." In light of Bible integration, that is a misleading phrase. All subjects are Bible subjects, from Bible geography and poetic books to God's principles of math in business and God's working with man in American history. Any material that is not viewed in study through the Word of God is potentially dangerous.

Facts as they relate to knowledge must be accompanied by understanding. This leads to godly wisdom. Students are not tanks to be filled with information. They are living spiritual organisms to be molded by God's direction. Secular humanists claim they give students facts and let them discover the use of them. The result is for them to do their own thing. That is deception. The curriculum is molded by an unrighteous teacher's point of view. That is also dangerous. It is akin to giving a loaded gun to a child with no instruction as to how to use it with safety. In the amoral setting of the secular world, that is an unacceptable limitation. But in Christian education we are committed to teach that which pleases God; "For the LORD giveth wisdom: out of his mouth cometh knowledge and understanding" (Prov. 2:6).

God's Children

In this conflict for control the greatest stake is our children. "Lo, children are an heritage of the LORD: and the fruit of the womb is his reward" (Ps. 127:3). We have already seen the result of state control with children academically and morally. The state says that the children are the property of the state, and this socialistic concept has swept across the land since the infamous International Year of the Child. In the state of Michigan a child protection law was adopted in 1975. The purported purpose was to protect the battered child. Every sensible person is against brutality to children. But now the law is applied arbitrarily to parents who use Biblical corporal punishment. This is accomplished by the "Children's Protective Services" being granted powers at the level of secret police. Instead of a protection for the child, it is a danger to the honest citizen who must obey the Bible.

In *Moody Monthly,* November, 1979, Gary Hardaway writes in "Will the Government Raise Your Child?"

> On the other hand, some campaign for maximum governmental intervention in families. Judge Lisa Richette of the First Judicial District of Pennsylvania says, "If there is a least detrimental alternative, remove the child and don't worry about the rights of the parents. The child belongs to society. The parents were only biological producers."[11]

As frightening as this sounds, it is true. The reader should be aware that "child abuse" is interpreted by the dictatorial Department of Social Services as any emotional, mental or religious abuse. The underlying warning is that the state is responsible for your little ones.

Children are made in the image of God and belong to God. We will not render them unto Caesar. God is the authority in the training of His children: "And all thy children shall be taught of the LORD; and great shall be the peace of thy children" (Isa. 54:13). The Lord's command in the teaching of these children is instruction in righteousness twenty-four hours a day for seven days a week (Deut. 6:6, 7).

Children have not always been viewed as property of the state by civil authorities as shown in a Supreme Court ruling.

> The fundamental theory of liberty upon which all governments in this Union repose excludes any general power of the State to standardize its children by forcing them to accept instruction from public education only. The child is not the creature of the State; those who nurture him and direct his destiny have the right, as well as the high duty, to recognize and prepare him for additional duties.
>
> This has rightly been recognized as an important decision, and it is probable that the distinguished Justice intended to express the very principle of the rights of parents and the limitations of the state in education which some enthusiastic readers have read into it.[12]

A growing claim by government to control children and families has led to a superimposed view of being God instead of speaking for Him. Here is the heart of the conflict. Does the state own your child, and can they force him to be educated in the state church (school)?

> The state is the collective representation of secularized man. But the state goes on to shape man himself by universal education, now extended even to maturity, fashioning him for its own type of nationalism and industrialism, in peace and in war. No wonder the most frequent issue in church-state relations is that of the purpose and method of education, whether youth is to be trained only by and for the state, or with some educative claim for God on the part of family and church.[13]

We maintain that in the matter of education, separation must be maintained without any violations or exceptions.

> . . . "Separation" means that there should be no contact between religion and government, and thus that public education should be altogether secular. Thus many others besides the Catholics fall under his displeasure. "Breaches in the wall of separation" are caused not only by those who clamor for free textbooks and bus rides for parochial school children, but also by those who seek to associate religion and public education in any way.[14]

Certainly there has been a two-sided error. We must correct this now. That requires a great deal of understanding and cooperation.

> One does not view the present relations of religion and education, in historical perspective, unless he realizes that the church, while the foster mother of learning, has also been the chief antagonist from whom teachers have had to wrest the freedom which they sought. Their present struggle for freedom is conditioned largely by the folklore and folkways of our political and economic order. The academic tenure of an anarchist or a communist is at least as precarious as that of an atheist. But the battle against clerical interference and coercion is still on and the propaganda of the churches against evolution and sex intelligence produces in the academic world an anti-religious attitude just as capitalistic pressure induces in the professional class a sympathy with economic radicalism. The psychology of conflict is not conducive to mutual appreciaton and understanding.[15]

Opposing Views

There are two opposing views. Both are a violation of law. (1) The state controls education, including the church school, with no physical assistance. (2) The church allows control and takes what it can in physical support. We support the view that there will be no government support of this church ministry of education and therefore no control. Civil power may neither support nor prohibit, by law or regulation, the church or any of her ministries.

You can see the battle lines forming. For the state, it is a determination to control or destroy. For the compromising religionist, it is to hang on as long as possible (ultimate destruction is guaranteed). For the modern, nonconforming Biblicist, there is *no* compromise, come victory or death. Russia accomplished this in her declaration of freedom of religion under the separation of church and state. "The school shall be separate from the Church. The teaching of religion is prohibited in all state, municipal or private educational institutions where a general education is given."[16] Those who have read current school laws may wonder where Russia obtained that one.

> Although firmly entrenched in America today, this secularized statist system is yielding to persistent efforts by freedom-loving, God-fearing Americans to re-establish private Christian schools where students are again being taught Biblical truths and principles on a daily basis. How great it is to be on the cutting edge of a movement that can reverse the trend toward moral and spiritual decadence and restore God's righteousness to the nation.[17]

The Bottom Line

The Christian school's miraculous growth has triggered a collision course. There is no way to avoid this. State school education cannot be cured. At this point in its degradation it would be unconstitutional to reenroll God. For that reason the state school will die a slow death. With no moral support every action is self-destructive. The state school will ultimately commit suicide. The next chapter explains the nature of this death.

Footnotes

1. Engel v. Vitale, 370 U.S. 421 (1962).

2. Timothy McNulty, "Church and State in a Life-and-Death Education Battle," *Detroit Free Press* (May 2, 1979), sec. C, p. 2.

3. "Terror in the Schools," *U.S. News & World Report*, (January 26, 1976), pp. 52-55.

4. Ibid., p. 54.

5. Jerry Williamson, *Is Your Child a Ward of the State Church?* (Fort Lauderdale: Gold Coast Christian School, n.d.), p. 3.

6. Henry M. Morris, *Education for the Real World* (San Diego: Creation-Life Publishers, 1977), p. 79.

7. William Barclay, *Educational Ideals in the Ancient World* (Grand Rapids: Baker Book House, 1959), p. 238.

8. Hall, p. 123.

9. Barclay, p. 247.

10. Morris, pp. 150-162.

11. Gary Hardaway, "Will the Government Raise Your Child?" *Moody Monthly,* (November 1979), p. 20.

12. Lee, pp. 13, 14.

13. Loetscher, p. 247.

14. Cuninggim, p. 132.

15. Hough, pp. 205, 206.

16. de Chalandeau, p. 122.

17. "From the Editor's Desk," *The Communicator* (September-October 1979), p. 3.

SEVEN

Taxation and the Church

"If it is evil for the state to support the church, it is equally as evil for the church to support the state" (Clay Nuttall).

ONE OF THE MOST misunderstood areas in the separation issue is taxation. Our premise is that under no circumstances should the church ever allow itself to be taxed. The power to license is the power to control. The power to tax is the power to destroy.

Confrontation

This is a very live issue as reported in the October 1979 issue of the *CLA Defender.*

> The Solono County, California tax assessor has sold the land and buildings of the Calvary Baptist Church of Fairfield to the State of California for taxes. The church suffered the foreclosure because of failure to sign the necessary tax forms. In California, a church must fill out and sign the exemption forms, or it loses its tax exempt status.[1]

This article goes on to explain some of the areas covered by the questions on the "Annual Information Statement." The church is forbidden to influence moral legislation or election of legislators.

This "gag law" tells the church to be silent where God has said to speak.

Several other churches in California face the same problem because they rightfully refuse to fill out these illegal forms. What the civil powers are saying is to forget God and do things their way or they will close the church.

I have before me ten pages of forms from the New York State Board of Equalization and Assessment. These forms are an application for real property tax exemption for nonprofit organizations and include required information on (a) organization purpose, (b) property use, (c) property as "parsonages" or "manses." An attached letter explains the mailing: "In compliance with the latest direction of the New York State Divison of Equalization and Assessment, we are enclosing application forms to be used by all nonprofit organizations claiming exemptions under Section 420 of the Real Property Tax Law." There is also an urgent note that the church comply as quickly as possible so that the application can be processed without delay.

It is interesting that the instructions do not mention who is to pay for having this bureaucratic monstrosity filled out. There is no explanation as to why the state feels free to violate constitutional law.

Another try at this kind of underhanded legislation was proposed in Michigan. House Bill 4177 was intended to discover the amount of nontaxable property churches hold. It did not, however, cover all nontaxable property, only that which the state wished to control. Nonprofit organizations would have to play "paper-work-patsy" or else be put on the tax rolls. A successful drive was mounted against this bill, and it was driven back to committee. The argument, by its supporters, was that it was not intended to tax churches, but this was a direct outcome of the bill. The nonconformists in the state had already informed the authors that the bill was in violation of constitutional law and that Bible-believing churches would not fill out the illegal forms.

This first illustration points out something of a radical change in the liberal tactics to destroy the church. The church is now being grouped with all "nonprofit" organizations. There may be no precedent for nonprofit groups, but the bureaucracy must treat the church separately because it operates on conviction, not on organization.

The reader may feel that liberal legislators and anti-American lobbyists are not too bright. They just will not take *no* for an answer. The people vote against something, the government does it anyway. The people protest, the government just keeps coming back with more offensive proposals. This is, of course, the tactic; keep it up and the people will give in and quit. This is a warning for those dishonest perpetrators of fraud. When they get up against the brand of dissidents that brought the First Amendment into being, they will think twice. "They won't bend, and they won't burn."

These Stories Came by the Hundreds

The Fundamental News Service passes along more horror stories. "Nine Barrington [Rhode Island] churches will be taxed on an estimated total of $12,863 when tax bills go out this summer, according to Mrs. Joyce Lewis, town tax assessor." Hartford, Connecticut, "Would exempt churches from the service charge [taxes], but would levy it on hospitals and private schools." That means if it is a church school, the church is taxed. "Eleven churches [Westbrook, Maine] maintaining parsonages will receive tax bills here for the first time." What is really sad is the comment by Beverly B. Farley, a member of the Board of Assessors, "We've had very little reaction from the churches so far."[2]

Fallacious Concepts

The above statement reflects the incredible ignorance and the apathy rampant in the church today. It is the purpose of this chapter to deal with those views that have set the church up for control, persecution and destruction.

The church is a collective body of believers. While individual Christians are to be submissive to the government, the church is an equal sovereign power in its own realm. The exemption of the home relative to government control is different from the exemption of the church. The reason for this is the collective ministry of the church. The paying of taxes is an act of submission. For the church to agree that the state is its authority in all matters is unacceptable.

> The proper function of government is to promote good in order that peaceable and godly lives may be lived (1 Tim. 2:2; Rom. 13:3). For this reason believers should pray faithfully for those who rule (1 Tim. 2:2), and be submissive to rulers (Rom. 13:1-7). Submission is required for four reasons: government is ordained of God, any resistance to government is in reality to God, government is for the good, and the conscience demands it. Submission will manifest itself in paying dues and custom taxes and in fear and honor of the rulers.[3]

To combat this destructive attitude among believers, let me list those areas of fallacious thinking.

1. *We ought to pay our own way as churches.* There is something dishonest about a church that uses the legitimate tax issue to hide behind. Paying for utilities such as water, sewer, garbage, heat and lights are without question the responsibility of the user. They are clearly measurable. But even in those areas, the church should not accept a tax listing. Every church leader who wishes to obey the Bible should refuse, under any circumstances, to allow the church to be placed on the tax rolls.

What do we do with immeasurable items, such as police protection? Here is a perfect example of the extreme prejudice of tax officials. In any active, evangelistic local church it can be demonstrated that the church provides more crime control for the community than the local law enforcement agency has provided for all of the churches in its jurisdiction. Think of all the lives transformed by the new birth who no longer are violators and who are delivered from acts of violence and judgment. At the cost of housing one prisoner, the service exchange is worthy. The church is the salt of the earth and the light of its community.

Add to the above the overt services of the church in caring for the needy, the elderly, the handicapped, the retarded and the orphans. The ministry of the church is a rising star in these areas. The illegal bureaucracies need to stop lumping the church with charitable organizations and limiting their ministry by harassment.

2. *We are obligated to obey all the law.* It is demonstrated in chapter 2 that this is not a Bible truth. There are times when a law is not a law and the church is obligated to politely refrain from participating, even if this means prison and death. We are never to deride the name of the Lord Jesus Christ Who is Head of the church.

The state does have the power to tax the individual citizen. There is nothing in Scripture, on the other hand, that permits the state to tax the church. The reasons for this are clear. The first is control. The second is ownership.

In Romans 13 we learned that the state may levy taxes on the individual. Tax money is the source of revenue for the state to wage war, punish criminals and protect "good works," including the ministry of the church. The church, however, is the recipient of the tithe. If all of God's people were spiritually honest, the state would not now be involved in the moral care of many segments of our society. Biblical rule and agreement of constitutional law is this: *None of the taxes should pass from the state to the church,* and *None of the tithe may pass from the church to the state.* This sharing of funds should not be done indirectly or directly. This means that the actual passing of those funds is diverted through someone or something else.

Not even the civil powers are free to embezzle money or to violate the law of the land. The point has come in this conflict where the church must obey the higher power.

3. *Tax exemption is a subsidy to the church.* This particular argument is clouded by the fact that many illegal subsidies have been granted religion. These need to be cared for lest the matter of tax exemption be included as a wrong direction in the conflict.

> Some post-World War II developments, however, have focused considerable attention on the whole matter of aid to religious activities by the government. If exemption from taxation is regarded as a form of aid, then the important thing today is not that the pattern exists—a fact conceded on all sides—but whether it can and should be continued.[4]

The establishment of tax exemption does not rest in our historical moorings alone. It is a Bible issue so that any change of direction needs to be taken from the source. The Old Testament Levite was treated with this special standing; likewise, all that came into the temple. We have noted in chapter 1 that even the heathen king, Artaxerxes, decreed ". . . that touching any of the priests and Levites, singers, porters, Nethinims, or ministers of this house of God, it shall not be lawful to impose toll, tribute, or custom, upon them" (Ezra 7:24).

We cannot ignore the historical background that declares that this has always been the standard. Where there was violation of this direction, the civil powers were looked upon with disdain.

In the book by Huegli on this subject, he comments:

> Thus far there has been no "establishment" of religion with the exemption pattern. Hence it is hard for most Americans to see in it a violation of the First Amendment. Any privilege granted is shared without discrimination by all churches, and church activity is regarded as important to the American way of life. There would therefore seem to be nothing improper about the exemption.[5]

Then why all the fuss? The fault in this quarrel lies at the feet of church leaders who know or care little about the precepts of God's Word on this subject. It is also a deliberate drive by the pagan mind in America to destroy every vestige of religion. This plagues that mind. Every time the sinner is reminded he is a sinner or that which he is proposing is godless, there is a strengthening drive to control that voice or, as in the case of John the Baptist, to destroy it. These natural men think that they can scare the church into compromise. How little they know of the history of the true church. There are nonconformists from here to Heaven.

This open conflict will bring to light many new areas of discussion over possible subsidized help from the government.

> The churches, or their religion, are recognized by law and by government custom in various public ceremonies and in observance of Sunday (*q.v.*). Chaplains are provided at public cost, not only for the armed services, but also for many prisons, hospitals, and public institutions. Church properties, whether defined strictly or most comprehensively, are exempted from general taxation. The exemption amounts in total to an enormous subsidy, increasing as rates of taxation are increased. Social security benefits are made available to important classes of church employees, and are accepted by many though not usually by clergymen.[6]

True to our stated convictions, if it is clearly demonstrated that there is direct or indirect passing of funds to the church, this must be corrected. These errors should not be used as a base to violate the First Amendment. The church should pay *no* taxes. The church should *never* be placed on the tax rolls. That is control and destruction. Civil power may make *no* law prohibiting the free exercise of religion. *No* law includes illegal tax laws.

Before we leave this area, the matter of exemptions needs to be handled. It is a broad area. The government does have the power to grant them. The question is, Are they viable in matters that pertain to income tax? Gifts to religious organizations and churches are legitimate at this time. We only reflect that it is not only legal, but it does seem just, in that the church is performing its God-directed functions preventing the state from getting involved. Furthermore, it is not a matter of funds exchanged or directed.

A real war wages, however, over deductions for religious education. Several states have had the court strike down voucher plans and such deductions. Others have already implemented them, such as Louisiana.

> Gov. Edwin W. Edwards has signed into law legislation which will provide state income tax credits for the 1979 taxable year to well over half a million Louisiana taxpayers . . .
>
> . . . As amended, the bill will provide a $25 tax credit per

child in public or nonpublic schools of Louisiana. A family with three children, for example, would have a credit of $75, which would be subtracted from the amount due on state income taxes for 1979.[7]

Of all the areas considered this one seems to be the clearest. To allow a deduction for church school education does not seem to violate the First Amendment. First, it is not an exchange of money. Second, it is a legitimate deduction in that while it is listed as tuition, it is not a payment. Payment for education has already been made through the forceable removing of education taxes by the state which has no precedent for the educating of God's people. The state schools have a poor track record in educating the children of the general society. They are obviously unable to educate the children of the church as God has commanded without violating the separation of church and state.

More serious yet is the Supreme Court ruling that humanism is a religion and that the public school is the major proponent of this religion. Added together, that makes the state-federal school an established state church.

If there is no way for a constitutional method to protect the parent's funds for education, one possibility remains. The government must cease taking education taxes and find a way for those funds to go directly from the parent to the school system. That may sound like a radical statement, but in view of increasing socialistic pressure there seems to be no alternative.

We are often told that parents who want special educational privileges should be quiet and pay for them. After all, we are told, education is provided. The answer is that the state cannot, should not and will not provide an education for the children of the church that is acceptable to Biblical standards. Here is another example of repression of religious freedom. "You can have your religious freedom if you want to pay twice for it." Parents are fined for obeying God. The answer is *no* to a state church which teaches and practices the religion of humanism.

4. *Churches compete with businesses and should be treated like them.* Let us be clear. No church should run a business. Those that do are in violation of the Bible and constitutional law. It is still wrong to tax the church at any level. Those churches ought to get out of those businesses. The problem is that many legitimate ministries of the church are being called into question. Where the church can demonstrate a direction of God for a ministry it should be free from control.

The statists are angry that the church is giving them competition in many areas that were once a monoply. They arbitrarily declare these are business areas and that the church does not belong in them. What a confession of their own hypocrisy.

A very important test is whether the disputed tax exemption is wealth producing or not. Strangely enough, the dictatorial bureaucracies are not going after those wealth-making arms of religion. The struggle is in the areas of ministries that are not and could not be profit making, i.e., church schools, day-care centers, camps, service ministries. These church ministries are not businesses; they are not profit making or wealth producing. The legitimate ministries of the church are in no sense comparable to a business.

5. *Churches which speak out on moral and political issues take advantage of tax exemptions.* This problem has already been mentioned. To review, let us remember that one of the major reasons the church is in the world is to speak out on such moral issues as those that crowd our legislature today. The church also has the responsibility to encourage the righteous to rule. When the wicked are in power, the cause of Christ always suffers. To penalize a church for obeying God is wrong.

An example of this intolerable atheistic conglomerate is in order. Suppose a church spoke out on legislation pertaining to abortion. The state illegally taxes its property as a result. The church in this case literally supports something that is against God as a conviction.

May God increase the number of the churches that will speak for Him in moral matters. The preachers of our day need to thunder like prophets of old until their voices are heard across the community and those wicked purveyors of murder and filth hide their faces in fear of the coming judgment.

This leads us to a final consideration. Does the government have the power to withdraw the tax-exempt status of a church? We concede that the state may have the power to enforce its illegal action, but we will never believe the state has the right or responsibility to do so.

At this time state agencies are using every excuse under the sun to violate the church. Some time ago the Internal Revenue Service tried to do that under the guise of punishing segregationists. In a book that every person interested in this subject should read, *Why Churches Should Not Pay Taxes,* this point is made.

> It is the thesis of this book that tax exemption is not something churches (or any nonprofit voluntary organizations, for

that matter) win by "good" behavior or lose by "bad" behavior, as "good" or "bad" may be defined at will by incumbent officials from day to day. Churches have their essential function to perform, which they do—and have done for decades and centuries—as best they can, and which outsiders, particularly government officials, cannot judge, and—even if they could—do not have the wisdom, means, or right to try to improve the churches' performance. Loss of tax exemption will not make poorly functioning churches function better, and the threat of it will only have a "chilling effect" on those that are not doing too well as it is, so that they will tend to falter and "lose their nerve" and do even less well.[8]

Our Answer Is No

Our answer to this perplexing question is *no.* The state does not grant tax exemption, it only recognizes it. Therefore the most horrible of legal atrocities is committed when a church is molested in such a manner. Whatever compelling interest the state may have, taxation is never an answer. It should be unacceptable to any Bible-believing church.

To those well-meaning but uninformed persons who advocate surrender of that which is Christ's to Caesar, one could only say, "You should know what does belong to Christ. If you are doing something other than what you should be doing as a church, close the whole thing down. If, however, your ministry and your church belong to Christ, even one dollar as a tax confesses that Christ is no longer Head of the church."

I challenge you, ". . . How long halt ye between two opinions? if the LORD be God, follow him: but if Baal, then follow him" (1 Kings 18:21). All of the Scripture that we referred to earlier (Matt. 17:27; 22:15-22; Mark 12:17; et al) are references to the individual responsibility to pay taxes. Biblically, historically and practically, the answer is *no,* the church should not defame the name of Christ by paying taxes.

Footnotes

1. "Tax Foreclosure Against California Baptist Congregation," *CLA Defender* (October 1979), p. 1.

2. B. Robert Biscoe, ed., *Fundamental News Service* (Valley Forge, PA: American Council of Christian Churches, n.d.), p. 2.

3. Charles Caldwell Ryrie, *Biblical Theology of the New Testament* (Chicago: Moody Press, 1959), p. 208. Used by permission.

4. Huegli, pp. 396, 397.

5. Ibid., p. 399.

6. Loetscher, p. 249.

7. "Louisiana Wins on Tax Credit Plan," *Freedom in Education* (July-August, September 1979), p. 3.

8. Dean M. Kelley, *Why Churches Should Not Pay Taxes* (New York: Harper & Row, 1977), pp. 131, 132.

EIGHT

Who May License the Church?

". . . Render therefore unto Caesar the things which are Caesar's; and unto God the things that are God's" (Matt. 22:21).

THE PLAN to destroy would include the plan to control; the plan to control would include the plan to license; and the plan to license would include the plan to regulate.

Head of the Church

In the case of the taxation, payment indicated submission. In the case of license, submission indicates headship. We need to get our premise recorded here. Jesus Christ is the Head of the church. "And he is before all things, and by him all things consist. And he is the head of the body, the church: who is the beginning, the firstborn from the dead; that in all things he might have the preeminence" (Col. 1:17, 18).

It is understood that a higher authority approves and licenses a lower. If the state licenses the church or any of its ministries, it has full power to violate the will of God, and that is just what is happening in our land today.

The direction involved is covered with a multitude of words: approve, license, accredit, certify. They all mean the same thing. In due time one bows down to Caesar even in the areas that are not his to regulate. Dr. Roy Thompson makes this crystal clear.

> Let's keep the issue simple, even though we live in a very complex society. If you must get a certificate or license, whether from the Department of Education, the police or fire departments, health and welfare, or whatever, it is still state control over the church. If they have the power to say you can, they have the power to say you can't, it is that simple. Until now, they never dared to do it to the church and still basically are not, but they are to the Christian school which should be as much a part of the Church as any other ministry.[1]

What is the reason behind this conflict between church and state? Is it the fault of some rabid fundamentalists who want to cause trouble? In actuality it is the same thing that brought persecution to the early church. Elgin Moyer in *Great Leaders of the Christian Church* lists three reasons for us: (1) rigid morality; (2) loyalty and devotion to Christ; (3) religious exclusivism. Because Christians separated from employments and diversions which involved heathen worship, superstition or immorality, they were considered "unsociable." Also, as they sought to be obedient to the Lord's command of making disciples of all nations, they became "offensive" to the Roman law. They used no images in their worship, and were considered "atheists." Because they refused to obey laws violating their consciences, they were considered "anarchists." They conducted unlicensed meetings and were regarded as "criminal." And, because they observed the Lord's supper, they were considered "cannibals."[2]

Compelling Interest

Among legal authorities in the Christian camp there seems to be an agreement that the state has certain compelling interests. These center around the safety of its citizens. The concern is how far do those interests of the state go? The bureaucracy in its present position evidently feels there are no limits. On the other hand, the courts are asking three questions: (1) Is it legitimate to safety? (2) Does it accomplish the end desired? (3) Is it uniform in its application?

The curse of bureaucratic hypocrisy is demonstrated here. Agency responsibilities come to us with that computer mentality that says, "Nothing personal, I am just doing my job." Sounds like echoes from Nazi gas chambers. When we confront these department people with their total inconsistencies, they say, "That's not my area." The court is not agreeing.

A good example is the application of fire codes. A church, for instance, operates for several years with five hundred people attending Sunday school—no problem. They begin a ministry to children, to youth, to adults—silence. Then they obey God and open a Monday-to-Friday school. The roof comes off, and they are dragged into court like common criminals. What was safe for five hundred on Sunday is now *unsafe* for fifty on Monday. This is a perfect illustration of why the church can never let the state license one of its ministries. We are being suffocated slowly and do not know it. "And that, knowing the time, that now it is high time to awake out of sleep: for now is our salvation nearer than when we believed. The night is far spent, the day is at hand: let us therefore cast off the works of darkness, and let us put on the armour of light" (Rom. 13:11, 12).

In a land where you are fined $5000 for destroying an eagle's egg and paid by welfare to kill your baby, it is not shocking that the humanist can no longer allow the voice of the church to be heard. The plan is simple: taxation, licensure and financial exhaustion in court. If that will not do, lock them in jail. Over fifty thousand murderers are loose on the streets with more being set free by our courts, and America's preachers are going to jail. In the words of Patrick Henry, "Great God, Great God, Great God!"

Areas of Encroachment

The best way of handling the content of this chapter is to list the areas of encroachment. These are not all the avenues of attack, but the major ones.

1. *Taxation.* We have already discussed this in the previous chapter. Tricking the churches and her ministries into applying for exemption is treachery. A good policy for defense is to never fill out report forms or requests. Tax deduction is the other area. The Internal Revenue Service attempted to put the church on the defensive and assumed the education ministry of the church as in violation until proven innocent.

When the sovereignty of the local church is broken by any of these subtle directions, there is no end to control even though every act violates the First Amendment.

2. *Labor Relations.* The question of organized labor in church ministries is now a fact. A roadblock has been placed in this path as a result of the U.S. Supreme Court decision (1979) holding that the

National Labor Relations Board has no jurisdiction over church-related schools. The decision was based on the constitutional separation of state and church; but, it is claimed, did not negate the right of church workers to organize.

In another example of this, the Seventh-day Adventist Church was forced to pay $650,000 in back wages to women teachers. It has refused to acknowledge the government's right to be involved in the case. This case, representative of the mid-70s, demonstrates the danger of Labor Department violations.

More critical than organized labor is the question of who tells a church whom they may employ. The September 1979 *Advocate* printed this headline, "Church Sued in Dismissal of Homosexual Staff Member." The problem of employee qualification is a grave one as we shall see in other areas.

One other point of concern is unemployment tax. Can the state require this of a church, any of its employees or any ministry? Our answer is *no*. That is unacceptable control. The state of Tennessee has done an about-face on this issue. Instead of persecuting churches, it is defending them.

> The case arose out of the ruling by Secretary of Labor Ray Marshall concerning the taxing of church schools. Mr. Marshall concluded that the teaching of academic, "non-religious" subjects is a secular activity and was subject to the unemployment tax. The Tennessee churches, along with many other Fundamentalist churches nationwide, resisted the ruling on the ground that the Government should not define the limits of a church's ministries.[3]

3. *Camp Safety*. Church camps will virtually be an impossibility under continued oppressive standards by both state and federal governments. Here is an excellent example of where the church should have drawn the line at compelling interests.

4. *Day Care*. The Hillsborough (Florida) County Commission recently voted to exempt church day-care centers from Florida statutes requiring control. This is another victory in a long struggle against the incompetency of bureaucrats. The Laodicean apathy of other churches is reflected in that most of the area's church day-care centers fell in line, like sheep to the slaughter, without a word.

This may be the best example of separation violation we have. First, this is a nonprofit ministry. Second, it is a justifiable ministry of the local church and an integral part of the total ministry.

With all of this in mind, one can evaluate the future stress on the church. The department of social services says it regulates employees (including the sandbox director); stipulates curriculum and materials, forbidding some (meaning the Bible); requires (to a nail) certain or all equipment. We are told by these representatives that if they can control a ministry of the church they can control the church. To make that clear, it means preacher, pulpit and buildings. To the doubters among my readers, go on to the next chapter and weep.

5. *Children's Homes.* Control in this area is nearly complete. Almost everyone has given in to illegal mandates. Those who have fought have had the bloodiest battle of all. We will discuss these in chapter 9. Scotty Drake of Tampa, Florida, exposed the "bureaucratic bungling" of the Division of Health and Rehabilitative Services in pointing out the filthy, dangerous conditions of their own facilities. The answer? "None of your business; don't do as we do—do as we say!"

6. *Special Interest Groups.* An example of this is the "Barrier-free Code Commission" set up in Michigan. The group was stacked with handicapped members and bitterly took on everyone in the state. When they came to churches, they commanded that the church make it possible for handicapped people to get anywhere on their own power, even if it meant a half-mile ramp to the baptismal pool. To be sure, many of our churches have failed here. Churches ought to do everything to bless our dear handicapped friends, but to the state we say, "Stop at the wall of separation."

7. *Health.* The state has a way of making church people look a little less than bright, and less than compassionate. Of course, we should be concerned about health. However, keeping the health department's records *for* them is another thing. Who can tell the church if it can have a kitchen, what size sink it may have, forbid potlucks (heresy!), and refuse a visitation dinner prepared in the church. The state health agents say they can. Did you know it is required in the state of Michigan that a church school interfere in the God-given rights of parents regarding immunization? Is there a legitimate compelling interest here? If there is, the state had better walk softly. Some church leaders are wise to this road.

8. *Education.* This writing has dealt in-depth with this section of the conflict. It was the catalyst that brought confrontation, and it included many other battlefronts as well. While in some measure the state boards of education have been embarrassed by their poor showing in the graduation lines, it appears that they are using other departments to do their dirty work. Michigan state senator Jack Welborn is quoted in a 1979 news report, "My feeling is that the

Department of Education is trying to close down private unfunded schools through fire marshals by selective enforcement of fire codes."[4]

This trend of the state is due partially to the overwhelming defeat of state education in Ohio. The record of this victory is found in *Ohio's Trojan Horse* by Alan N. Grover. I like his declaration on page 117.

> When in the course of human events, it becomes necessary for Christian people, who are God-fearing and law-abiding citizens, to refuse to comply with the bureaucratic regulations promulgated by the State Board of Education, and to maintain the doctrine known as "separation of church and state," which the laws of our land have established, and which accords with the church polity taught in the Christian Scriptures, a decent respect to the opinions of all concerned requires that they should declare the causes which impel them to the maintenance of this separation.[5]

A warning to everyone who is keeping count: This ministry of our churches is supposedly regulated by law—who we can hire, how long we can minister and what we will teach. If it can be done here, it will be done in all the ministries of the church.

Dare we warn you that this is the sacred cow? The humanists have a plan for God's children. They are to be delivered from parents, churches and Christian schools; these "child abusers" who believe in spanking. To whom will they deliver them? The advocates of child rights will bring them to the "utopia" of no discipline, lawlessness, drugs, sex, devil music and the loss of God's heritage.

Perhaps state boards of education are not able to use the devious route, then what? Truancy laws are next in an attack on the parents. Many of these critical cases already are in litigation.

I sat in a courtroom in Allegan, Michigan. A mother and father were on trial for educating their children in the sanctity of a religious home. The state could not and did not debate the excellent curriculum and good teaching (well qualified). The results of their teaching were unquestionable. Those parents may go to jail, however! Why? They were not state approved.

9. *Fire Marshal.* The hottest subject on the stove at the point of this writing is in this area. A real concern for the safety of children or adults is not the issue. "Safe on Sunday but not on Monday" is the issue. The conflict here again is the building approval; safe but not approved.

10. *Zoning*. This last path by the state is the most interesting of all. In some cases, such as Roy Forrest's in Concord, New Hampshire, the building was zoned as acceptable for intended use by the church until it opened a school. Of course it is just another ministry of the church, but the city fathers said, "Close the school or go to jail." The church won after much pain. However, the powerful state had injured the work of God, if only temporarily.

The illustration I wish to use here is about the Solon Baptist Temple in Solon, Ohio, pastored by Marion Wojnarowski. This young church suffered local government interference in the areas of fire safety and zoning. I wrote a letter of encouragement to the pastor about the time our church also faced court trial. At that time I also wrote a letter to the mayor of that city and received a response from him. I have recorded all of this correspondence because it shows the mentality of the civil government better than anything else could.

July 3, 1979

Rev. Marion Wojnarowski
2910 Tuxedo Ave.
Parma, Ohio 44139

Dear Brother,

A note of encouragement. Believe me we can sympathize with your heartache there in the City of Solon. We too have had great difficulty with the local government and have found ourselves in court August 7th and 8th. Our God is able to deliver both of us. Our prayers are with you. Be encouraged and keep looking up.

Maranatha,

Rev. Clay Nuttall
Sr. Pastor

July 3, 1979

The Honorable Charles Smercina
Mayor, City of Solon
6315 Som Center Road
Solon, Ohio 44139

Dear Sir:

For several months we have been receiving newsclippings in relationship to a difficulty that a local church has been having in your city. May I say that I find the news articles incredible. It seems that in the United States of America where we are guaranteed the separation of church and state, and freedom of religion, that any church could be oppressed for any reason.

I respectfully submit that if anything that we have read in the news articles is true, I want to plead with you and the community leaders to support religious freedom in our United States of America and in your city. It should never be the purpose of one church or denomination or one religion or the state to interfere at any level for any reason with the ministry of a local church even though we may feel that they are not a duly recognized local church. Sir, the day may come when all of our churches of all religions face the same persecution and oppression at every level.

I beg of you to consider very carefully the fact that the Pastor of the church of which I speak is a man anointed of God. It is extremely unwise to raise our hands against God's appointed ones.

I thank you for your time.

Sincerely yours,

Rev. Clay Nuttall
Sr. Pastor, Chr. Council of 13—Assoc. of Reg. Baptist Churches

July 11, 1979

Reverend Clay Nuttall
Sr. Pastor, Chr. Council of 13
Association of Reg. Baptist Churches
Fruitport Bethel Baptist Church
213 Oak Street
Fruitport, Michigan 49415

Dear Reverend Nuttall:

Thank you for the time that you took to advise me of your feelings with regard to the Solon Baptist Temple.

Solon is a fine community of decent, upstanding, and God-appreciative people. It is not now, and never has been our intent to harm or harass anyone, least of all a church.

Safety—PUBLIC SAFETY—is our only concern. We are faced with approximately 40 violations of the Ohio Building

Code and Fire Prevention Code in the use of the house. Law and common sense insist that we cannot ignore these safety violations.

My oath of office charges me to uphold the law and faithfully, honestly and impartially perform my duties and ends with "so help me God." I'm sure you would not want me to do less.

We are anxious to work with and cooperate with the Pastor so that the Temple can be made safe for all persons who will come there in good faith.

Sincerely,

Charles J. Smercina
Mayor

CJS/Jo
Enclosure
cc: The Herald Sun
The Solon Times
Council
Planning Commission

Following is the enclosure from *The Solon Times,* September 21, 1978, page 8.

'Settle Temple Differences'

The willingness expressed by a representative of the Solon Baptist Temple Monday to meet with the city's building commissioner and fire inspector is a welcome step in the right direction.

Five weeks ago, when these pages first reported violations of building and fire codes in the Temple—a frame house on SOM Center Road—we urged church officials to comply with regulations. Why has this agreement to meet taken so long?

While we recognize and support the church's First Amendment rights to exist without interference from government, we also know that building and fire codes for places of assembly exist for the welfare and safety of persons who occupy buildings. Church officials should be intent on meeting or exceeding such regulations, not reluctant to do so.

We hope the agreement to meet will produce a speedy end to this controversy. However, regulations made for safety purposes are not open to negotiation.

It is hard to understand the harassing letters Solon's mayor has received from clergymen as a result of his carrying out of administrative duties. This type of namecalling—"ungodly, satanistic and communistic"—normally does not come from religious people.[6]

'Is Baptist Temple Safe?'

This Sunday when the Rev. M. Wojnarowski conducts his services at the Solon Baptist Temple on SOM Center Road, his congregation will probably be as safe as any other.

Probably! But what if they aren't? The building is a house. It was constructed for occupancy by a single family, not by a congregation totaling 40 or more members. There are many building and fire regulations that must be met when a building is to be used as a place of assembly.

Wojnarowski claims the building is safe. He cites exits, fire extinguishers and fire signs as being adequate. But the building has not been inspected by the state as is required by law. The city's law director says a number of regulations have not been complied with.

Solon Building Commissioner Arthur Korkowski has an important job to do, and from indications we have received, he does it to the best of his ability.

We find charges of harassment leveled against Korkowski a little hard to swallow. Charges that First Amendment rights are being violated skirts the issue.

Once the building is inspected and, when it complies with applicable laws, the Solon Baptist Temple will be welcomed to the community as many other churches have in the past.[7]

July 17, 1979

The Hon. Charles J. Smercina
The City of Solon
6315 SOM Center Road
Solon, Ohio 44139

Dear Sir:

Please let me apologize. I ask forgiveness for any unkindness from fellow pastors. I looked over my letter to you. I do not feel I was unkind to you as a person; if I was, please tell me.

It would help you to be patient with these "men of God" if you knew that many of them and their godly peers have been in jail in our free America because the state has made laws and regulations that would keep them from obeying God's clear Biblical commands.

It would also help you to know that in the U.S. the state and church are equal authorities. The state is not over God. A church may meet anywhere at any time it wishes without any interference from the state. If someone is killed, etc. then the church leader who is responsible can be prosecuted for manslaughter by the state. This is called "the separation of church and state." You understand that when a dictatorial bureaucracy tells a church they may not meet until they lower a ceiling or put in an exit sign, they have made a law that violates the church and is in fact, the licensing of a church, which is forbidden by our Constitution.

Please, Mayor, be patient with these men whose very freedom is at issue. They hear of Christians in Russia who are imprisoned because they meet in a home. Obviously, they feel the same about regulations that violate our freedom in America.

Throughout church history this has been a problem, but the church will continue to meet in caves, basements and homes even if they go to jail or are killed. I agree that the church's standard should be higher than others, and in the main they are. The way to accomplish that is to respect the fact that a church is autonomous. Encourage them to make right decisions, but do not demand where God has not given (and our Constitution does not recognize) the state authority over the church.

Thank you for your consideration. I do not feel this letter is a personal attack on you. It clarifies our view of your God-given responsibility. We support that.

Sincerely yours,

Rev. Clay Nuttall, Sr. Pastor
Council Chairman, Mich. Assoc. of Regular Baptist Churches

Zoning is a serious consideration, for in some planned communities only a certain number of churches are permitted.

> But some zoning codes have recently followed a trend toward restricting or excluding churches in residential areas. On such cases brought before them, most state courts have refused to allow the exclusion, on the grounds that exclusion is

either a violation of the "due process' clause of the Fourteenth Amendment or of the "equal protection" clause of the same amendment. Not all courts agree, however, and a number have upheld exclusionary zoning.[8]

The Church of Jesus Christ is bound to take the gospel to the whole world. That includes those areas zoned to exclude or limit churches. The implication of this last item is astronomical.

Questions Being Asked

With a mind to those who will consider our view radical, let me answer some questions.

1. *What do we have to hide?* Nothing, but that is not the issue. How we share our information and who may command our disclosure is everything. No licensing body has that kind of power over the local church.

2. *Shouldn't we have the best?* Certainly, but who can tell us what we shall have and how we shall use it? That is the real question. We must not violate a higher law to please a lower intrusion.

3. *What shall I do? My people don't want to fight.* Pastor, preach the Word. Warn your people! Call them to responsibility. If we do not hang together now, we will hang separately later.

4. *Don't we want to attain to state standards?* Absolutely not. The standards of the church need to be much higher, and in most cases they are. It is not the legitimate standards we protest, but those that prohibit the free exercise of religion.

5. *We don't have a camp or Christian school. How does this affect us?* If this conflict is not won now, all church ministries are at stake. Like this one: "Vacation Bible School Ruled Illegal in Canada" (*CLA Defender*, September 1979). This tidal wave of licensure is sure to include the Sunday school and ministries of the gospel. If the licensed preachers are approved, who will be the unapproved ministers . . . shades of John Bunyan.

When the state of Virginia first announced that "a Sunday school conducted by a religious institution, or a facility operated by a religious organization . . . fits the definition of a child-care center as defined by the Code of Virginia" (*CLA Defender*, January 1979, p. 26), preachers shuddered. Then came the revelation that Alabama law and Michigan law had almost the same provisions. How do we know how many other states have done this?

A majority of church leadership would say, "They better not try to license my Sunday school." Fellow leader, the only thing left is to implement the code. If you stand by and let them violate constitutional law by regulating church school employees and curriculum, they *will* regulate the preacher and the pulpit.

Rendering unto Caesar

I have not forgotten that God has assigned certain responsibilities to the state. That, however, is not the purpose of this discourse. Dr. Don Boys cites this for us.

> Christians are law-abiding people. That is part of our nature and our teaching. Jesus said, in Matthew 22:21, ". . . *Render therefore unto Caesar the things which are Caesar's; and unto God the things that are God's.*" That means, we pay our taxes, vote, obey the law and generally do what good citizens do. It does not mean the state owns us, nor does it mean the state is our god. It is a sin not to give Caesar what is due him, but it is also a sin to give Caesar what belongs to God. The big problem in many states is that Caesar is trying to tell Christians what belongs to God and what belongs to Caesar. We can never permit that.[9]

This same author records his basis for such a belief and balances it with the Bible and law.

> The states are trying to license churches and schools as they would plumbers, lawyers, physicians and auto mechanics. Just a little problem here. They have no authority to regulate churches. The authorities don't like to hear that, but there can be no compromise for temporary safety. It must be clear to all. The state has assumed power it does not have relating to licensure of churches and Christian schools. The Constitution says, "Congress shall make no law." What was that? "No law."[10]

In the matter of licensing for control we are determined to obey God. ". . . Render unto Caesar . . . ;" pay your taxes, obey the speed laws, be a good patriotic citizen. There is no conflict with God for He gave this command. But "render unto God the things that are God's." What is God's?

Our children belong to God (Ps. 127:3). His image, not Caesar's, is stamped on them (Gen. 1:26). The state may not kidnap them or educate them. Our churches are Christ's. He is the Head of them. The tithe is the Lord's. We will not render any of it to Caesar through the tax. Our church staff members are saved and called of God. We will not render them for Caesar's secular approval. Our curriculum is the Bible (it is His Word), and we will not render it except to our God. Why?

> The Bible, and especially the New Testament, teaches the separation of church and state. God, the Sovereign Ruler, has delegated specific responsibilities and limitations of government to civil governments on one hand, and to church governments on the other hand. The government of the state is one government—to which the Christian must submit, with certain limitations. . . . The government of the church is an entirely separate government, established by God, and to which the Christian must also submit (see Hebrews 13:7; 1 Corinthians 6:1-5; 1 Peter 5:2, . . .). The Lord Jesus Christ taught that Christians must give submission both to civil government and to God's government, and that we must recognize the limitations of the government of the state. He said: ". . . Render therefore unto Caesar the things which are Caesar's; and unto God the things that are God's (Matthew 22:21)."[11]

A License Disaster

I close this chapter with one more warning about the deceitful level that liberals will stoop to in making sure they get their way. In 1979 a man named Jim Jones led over nine hundred followers to death, most of them suicides and all in one day. Guess who got the blame for the deaths of these members of the People's Temple in Guyana? "Jonestown has become a symbol of what fanatic fundamentalists will do if they are not licensed, controlled and approved."

The truth, of course, never came through the liberal press. Jones was not a fundamentalist, not a Christian; in fact, not even a religious person in the true sense of the word. He was a charlatan, a moral deviate and a Marxist. Jonestown was a political body, communistic at that.

Faith for the Family summarizes this crowd and their false messiah.

> Jones had no use for the Word of God or its teachings. . . . Throwing his Bible to the ground he stamped on it . . . "destroy this paper idol." . . . He claimed that he himself was the reincar-

> nation of Jesus Christ. . . . Jones' claims to extraterrestrial origin had special appeal to this Jonestown flock. . . . Wife, Marcelean, claimed that her husband adopted Christianity in order to prepare the people for Marxism. . . . He boasted that he would bring Communism to America. . . . Marxist Guyana was chosen as the site for the Jonestown community. . . . [He] planned to transport Jonestown to the Soviet Union as soon as the Russians gave their approval.[12]

This is not an example of fundamentalist anything. Here is a man who brandished recommendations from Rosalynn Carter, Mondale, Jackson, Humphrey and other political celebrities. Blame this one on the people of the state. Licensing never looked so bad.

Footnotes

1. Roy Thompson, "It's Still Licensure," *CLA Defender* (June 1978), p. 11.
2. Elgin Moyer, *Great Leaders of the Christian Church* (Chicago: Moody Press, 1951), p. 49. Used by permission.
3. "State of Tennessee Preparing Case Against U.S. Labor Department," *CLA Observer* (October 1979), p. 3.
4. Teri Banas, "Warrant Asked for Minister by Prosecutor," *Plymouth Observer* (October 22, 1979), p. 1.
5. Grover, p. 117.
6. "Settle Temple Differences," *The Solon Times* (September 21, 1978), p. 8.
7. "Is Baptist Temple Safe?" *The Solon Times* (September 21, 1978), p. 8.
8. Huegli, pp. 402, 403.
9. Donald G. Boys, *Liberalism: A Rope of Sand* (Indianapolis: Good Hope Press, 1979), p. 103.
10. Ibid., p. 102.
11. Grover, p. 107.
12. Dean Hallberg, "Jonestown—Background and Backlash," *Faith for the Family* (November 1979), pp. 3, 4.

NINE

The Preacher's in Jail

". . . We ought to obey God rather than men" (Acts 5:29).

IT WILL BE the purpose of this section to demonstrate the widespread abuse by the state and its agencies. We have insisted that the direction in the present civil government is to separate the church from the government while deliberately attaching the state to the church. Bureaucrats have had the audacity to disclaim harassment, abuse and open persecution of the church. The record will stand that in every one of these instances the state, to some degree, is in violation of the First Amendment.

For state violators to deny any offense or to claim protection of the law does not clear them; it only solidifies the claim of dissidents. It is not the persecuted who are uncooperative, but those who interfere in the Biblical and legal ministry of these churches.

They Dared to Obey God

The record shows that not all civil powers are unreasonable; some willingly obey constitutional law. Where the government does not violate God, we are *commanded* of God to obey them. Our children and our children's children will not say of these, "They were lawbreakers, and defied the legitimate legal process." Our heritage will say of these men and women as we have said of the nonconformists of the past two thousand years, "They dared to obey God."

For those who view these patriots as lawbreakers, I beg patience. In many cases, the church leaders went to agencies to ask for variances. When they were illegally refused and continued the ministry that is commanded of God, they were arrested for a religious activity. In the court they were asked, "If you did not think the state was in control, why did you ask for a variance?" The only way to obey God's dictates is to go into all the world. A believer does not need a variance to do God's will.

The following reads like a hall of fame. In some places it sounds like Foxe's book on Christian martyrs.[1] These cases do not come from the U.S.S.R., even though there are many parallels. These acts of travesty and injustice took place in America. Our forefathers shed blood to gain religious freedom. This book is a cry to the comfortable spirit, the apathetic mind, the fearful leader. Read and heed these accounts or we may have to shed our blood to keep our freedom.

Obviously, the inclusion of names, places and churches does not mean an approval of their total conduct, attitude, denominational affiliation or direction. If your fellowship does not have sensitivity to see the implications that these acts have on your stripe, these words are mundane anyway.

This is only the tip of the iceburg. However, they will serve as documented illustrations.

Random Illustrations

Zoning. Can the civil government zone property as to make illegal an integral ministry of a church?

Concord, New Hampshire: New Testament Baptist Church (Pastor Roy Forrest).

This is the story of a church and pastor who were rudely treated by local officials. In an attempt to work out the disagreements they fell into a satanic trap. When ordered to close a ministry of the church or go to jail, they refused. Support of fellow pastors, a rally and an appeal to the state Supreme Court ended in a just verdict. "The issue in this zoning case is whether a five-day-a-week school run by a fundamentalist church is a facility usually connected with a church. We hold that it is. . . . We hold that the Heritage Christian School is a proper permitted use connected with, and is part of the New Testament Baptist church."[2]

Education. Can the state tell a church that it cannot obey God in educating its children in the church, no matter how small its ministry?

Harvey, North Dakota: Victory Baptist Church (Pastor Peter Dyck).

In this case a pastor and his wife, by conviction, enrolled their children in their church school. The charges were brought against them under the Compulsory Attendance Law. "The father, Peter Dyck, has willfully refused to take his children to the Harvey Public Schools, the school that the children should attend." The charge was not that they were not being educated, but that they were not a part of the humanist educational monopoly. It is recorded that his six-year-old son awoke the night before the trial and cried out, "Please don't let them take my daddy to jail."

The trial was a perfect illustration of the weakness of humanistic education and the triumph of God's method. It ended when the court gave a directed verdict and acquitted Pastor Dyck. Because of some technical problem, this issue may reoccur.[3]

Education, Health, Building. Is a Christian school required to interfere with rights of parents in matters of health records and immunization?

Highland County, Florida: Sebring Academy (Dr. Kye Harris, Dr. Dan Frodge).

These two men went to jail rather than offend their conscience. The concern behind this case may receive more criticism, but no one can deny it happened. The case was taken to the Florida Supreme Court. The men were released.[4]

Child Discipline. Who owns the child? Is following Scripture for corporal punishment a crime?

Syracuse, New York (Pastor James Roy).

Fourteen-year-old Shirley Roy was forceably removed from her parents. The story of intrigue and abuse by the child protection agency is frightening. The civil agents demanded that the girl have a normal life (such as dancing and rock music).[5]

Children's Home. Does a ministry of a church have to be licensed when that violates the sovereignty of a local church?

Tampa, Florida: Good Shepherd Baptist Church (Pastor Scotty Drake).

This conflict has received national attention. The battle has been a long one. Here is a case where the state agency has one standard and demands another of the churches. Drake has faced jail more than once. The conflict is not over.[6]

Fire Code, Education. Does the church need any agency or department to approve its ministry?

Tujunga, California: Baptist Church of the Foothills (Pastor Ed White).

The fire inspector determined that the church must apply for and accept a Certificate of Occupancy. The agency claims the right to separate a school ministry from the church. The courts ruled the statute cited was invalid as applied to this case.[7]

Day Care. Can the state demand the power to license any ministry of a local church?

Seymour, Indiana: Seymour Baptist Temple (Pastor Martin Jones).[8]

Education. Who owns the child? Does the state have a right to force parents to use humanistic education when the authorities admit the child is receiving "superior education" in a religious school?

Richland County, Ohio (James Olin).[9]

Certification, Accreditation Standards. Does the state have the right to regulate private, church-related schools?

Frankfort, Kentucky: Twenty Christian Schools, Kentucky Association of Christian Schools.

The court said state interest "does not outweigh the school's First Amendment right to free exercise and expression of religion" and "quite the contrary, the overwhelming weight of substantial, probative evidence conclusively shows the state's effort to be but poorly conceived, ill-defined and quite direct interference with plaintiff's religious liberty."[10]

Christian Education. Does a church school have to be approved by the state?

Louisville, Nebraska: Faith Baptist Church (Pastor Everett Sileven, Pastor Edgar Gilbert).

The state in this case admitted that the children were receiving a superior education. Outcome pending.[11]

Zoning, Fire Code. Can the state forbid a church to meet, by zoning or fire code exclusion? (See chapter 8.)

Solon, Ohio: Solon Baptist Temple (Pastor Marion Wojnarowski).

Spanking. Can the state control the legitimate use of corporal punishment in church ministries?

Neilsville, Wisconsin: Bible Baptist Christian School (Teacher, Cynthia Webster).

Teacher charged with abuse of children; jury trial, possible term.[12]

Day Care. Is a ministry to children of the church required to be licensed by the state?

Hillsboro County, Florida: Good Shepherd Baptist Church, Providence Baptist Church, Temple Heights Baptist Church, Grace Bible Church.

This three-year dispute rejected on the prejudice of civil authorities. The county commission finally voted for the religious freedom of the churches and exempted them.[13]

Christian School. Can the state require a church to license its ministries?

Marshall, Texas: Grace Baptist Church (Pastor David Ashford).[14]

Passing Gospel Tracts. Can government limit evangelism?

Benton, Arkansas: Mike Sauvageot, Tim Murnay.

These boys were fined $500 each and sentenced to thirty days in jail. Charges have been dismissed.[15]

Taxation. Can the state tax a church for any reason?

Fairfield, California: Calvary Baptist Church (Pastor Harry Jackson).

The Solono County, California, tax assessor has sold the land and buildings of the Calvary Baptist Church. The church refused to sign illegal forms requiring the church to apply for tax exemption.[16]

Education. Can a civil government forbid a church from having a vacation Bible school?

Barrie, Ontario, Canada: Heritage Baptist Church (Pastor LeRoy Pennell).

This one did. The attorney for the township wrote, "Accordingly we take the position that the Bible school should not be operated within that building. Just as in the case of the day school, the vacation Bible school was viewed as a 'second use.' "[17]

Christian Education, Fire Code. Can the state select one ministry of the church and treat it independently?

Plymouth, Michigan: Central Baptist Temple (Dr. Stanley Jenkins).

A new school was opened in an established church. A state

senator charged the fire marshal was a front man for the board of education and that they were deliberately trying to shut down private schools. Officials failed to be embarrassed, even though they thought the building was safe on Sunday for a large group but unsafe on Monday for a small group. A shocking headline in the local Plymouth paper read, "Warrant Asked for Minister by Prosecutor."[18]

Licensing. Does state interest overrule religious liberty in the care of young people?

Corpus Christi, Texas: Rebekah Homes (Lester Roloff).

More people disagree over this case than probably any other. The issue is simple. Roloff takes nothing from the state and refuses their license. The Department of Human Resources appears to demand such control that they will fight to the death. This road through the courts has led to jail, appeal and the United States Supreme Court. On October 2, 1978, the Supreme Court said, "The appeal is dismissed for want of a substantial federal question." In the summer of 1979 Rebekah Home was still open and preachers from all over America joined together for a stand-off with the Department of Human Resources. There are many tragedies in the conflict.

One of the greatest problems of the state's view is exemplified in a statement that "what followed was one of the most remarkable exercises in civil disobedience in the state [Texas] history," when in actuality every witness said the stand-off was peaceful, quiet and legal.[19]

Education, Zoning, Health, Fire Code. Can the state apply one set of rules to the church in general and another set to a ministry of that church?

Battle Creek, Michigan: Liberty Baptist Church (Pastor David Lee).

A young church opened a new school and was faced with officials who felt the children should attend the available state institution. Outcome of trial is pending.[20]

Education. Does a church school have to meet the humanistic standards of an arbitrary set of "minimum standards"?

Darke County, Ohio: Tabernacle Christian School (Pastor Levi Whisner).

The Reverend Whisner, the pioneer of Ohio, stood by his religious freedom and the First Amendment. The Ohio Supreme Court agreed and awarded a landmark victory to him.[21]

These random illustrations only represent a portion of the conflict. We have not mentioned Georgia, Alabama, Virginia, North Carolina, Tennessee, Iowa or Washington—all of which have serious documented cases in litigation. What all of this does indicate for us is that we should be warned of a growing conflict.

Danger to the Home

The church is not the only area of difficulty. The home has felt this pressure in a real way. The cover of the *CLA Defender* of June 1978 shows state agents forceably removing children from their homes. If the sensitive person did not know better, he might believe that picture to be of KGB agents behind the Iron Curtain. On the first page of that same issue the mother is hauled away with no concern for her personal modesty.

In Michigan, my home state, the cities of conflict are growing: Fruitport, Battle Creek, Allegan, Plymouth, Iron Mountain, Pellston and Midland. Nearly forty Christian schools report threats.

Thank God for our country, our freedom and privileges to minister. We should be grateful for the moral leadership that does exist in our government. May their tribe increase. Let us be loyal, patriotic Christians. Patriotism and loyalty breed truth.

For emphasis, I repeat, I am not a pessimist, but a realist. These things are rehearsed because so many are uninformed. Too many are scoffers. Our brothers face heartache, and you may be next.

Footnotes

1. John Foxe, *Foxe's Christian Martyrs of the World* (Chicago: Moody Press, n.d.). Used by permission.
2. "City of Concord vs. New Testament Baptist Church—Heritage Christian School," *CLA Defender* (March 1978), p. 1.
3. Ibid., pp. 7, 8.
4. Dan Frodge and Kye Harris, "Why We Went to Jail," *CLA Defender* (August 1979), pp. 5, 6.
5. Earl Little, "The CLA Briefcase," *CLA Defender* (March 1979) p. 14.
6. Diane Sanchez, "Freedom Rally," *The Flaming Torch* (January 1979), pp. 1, 2.

7. "Victory Rings in Tujunga, California," *CLA Defender* (December 1978), p. 12.

8. Indiana Impact," *CLA Defender* (March 1978), p. 12.

9. "Bd. of Ed. vs. James Olin," *CLA Defender* (November 1978), p. 7.

10. John Cooley, "Victory in Frankfort," *CLA Defender* (November 1978), p. 7.

11. "Nebraska Update," *CLA Defender* (August 1979), p. 29.

12. "Briefcase: Wisconsin," *CLA Defender* (October 1979), p. 12.

13. "Tampa Suit Settled," *CLA Defender* (October 1979), p. 4.

14. "Update: Marshall, Texas," *CLA Defender* (January 1979), p. 16.

15. "Update: Benton, Arkansas Westside Baptist Church Victory," *CLA Defender* (January 1979), p. 16.

16. "Tax Foreclosure against California Baptist Congregation," *CLA Defender* (October 1979), p. 1.

17. "Vacation Bible School Ruled Illegal in Canada," *CLA Defender* (September 1979), pp. 1, 2.

18. "Warrant Asked for Minister by Prosecutor," *Plymouth Observer* (October 22, 1979), p. 1.

19. Dan Whisner, "That Is the Question," *CLA Defender* (August 1979), pp. 1, 2.

20. David D. Lee, Liberty Baptist Church, Battle Creek, Michigan, personal letter to Clay Nuttall, Fruitport Bethel Baptist Church, Fruitport, Michigan, October 15, 1979.

21. State v. Whisner, 47 Ohio St. 181 at 213, 214 (1976).

TEN

It Couldn't Happen Here

"You are hereby notified . . . any person with an interest in this land has a right to be heard at the circuit court hearing authorizing the tax sale" (Muskegon County Circuit Court, Michigan).

THIS FINAL CHAPTER is the record of what happened in my life and our church. Since the court trial has passed, these things are not philosophical. The distance was not great—only nine miles to the Muskegon County Courthouse. These pages will help the reader see why I speak without bitterness but with conviction, concern and growing alarm.

The Need for Pure Water

Fruitport, Michigan, is a small community. I was born in a house seven miles from the Bethel Baptist Church where I am senior pastor. For years the community had worked to get city water. The area water table was so contaminated that for years my family carried water until it could be piped in. The year before water came, the ground source became so bad that the well water could not even be used for washing.

Finally, a successful program was mounted, and pastors and people were happy to support the water authority. We had no idea that the thing which had brought us so much joy would bring us so much sorrow.

The township water authority assessed each of the parsonages one family unit and assessed the church thirty units for a total of $31,500. That was a lot of money, but the people were excited about having water and were willing to pay it.

On July 22, 1975, the township board, for reasons of its own, called a public hearing and adopted a resolution to reduce all church property assessments to two units. That would be a total of $2,100, a reduction of twenty-eight units. The people were jubilant and felt God had blessed their willingness to accept the larger assessment by faith.

The notice of the public hearing in the newspaper stated that "the assessments against the church-owned properties be reduced to two units each." On August 4, 1975, we received an official notice stating that, because of the special hearing on July 22, 1975, "it was determined at that time all churches would be reduced to two units for the property upon which your church is situated."

An Illegal Assessment

After this, a billing to a Grace Evangelical Lutheran School was sent to our church. That billing was returned to the township office. Later we were informed that an assessment of eight units ($8,400) had been made against one of our ministries, the Christian day school.

The day school, like all other equal ministries of the church, has no staff, no office and owns no books or equipment. It is truly an integral part of Bethel Baptist Church. Our associate pastor, Bob Rohm, and I visited the chairman of the water committee and the township supervisor. We explained that the school ministry does not legally exist and owns no property. This equal ministry had been assessed with all the others under the church assessment. We explained that it was not a question of money but of basic principle.

A letter dated October 9, 1975, from the township supervisor stated that the assessment would stand. Conferences with a local attorney left us with one recourse. On December 8, 1975, Pastor Rohm informed the township that the assessment was improper and illegal. Another letter followed on December 22, 1976. However, there was no response from the township.

The following year (1977), along with the illegal tax bill for the school ministry, Pastor Rohm sent a letter of explanation. There was a response to our letter, but it was the plan of the water department to add the school assessment to the total church, one which was also illegal. Each year a letter was forwarded to the township, but no headway was made.

Sale of Our Properties

Following Michigan tax guidelines, 1979 would be the year the delinquent tax properties would be sold. However, it was still a surprise when the Court notice came.

> Sir:
>
> You are hereby notified that the annual tax sale of lands for delinquent taxes of 1976, and prior years for the county of Muskegon will be made at the county treasurer's office of said county seat of said county, on the 1st day of May, 1979. According to the records of this office the following described lands are assessed to you and certain years' taxes thereon appear to be unpaid.
>
> If the taxes on the below mentioned lands are not paid prior to the date upon which said sale is to be held, then said lands will be sold for the taxes stated. Any person with an interest in this land has a right to be heard at the circuit court hearing authorizing the tax sale. This hearing will be held on the 12th day of March, 1979 at 10:00 A.M., at Circuit Court, County Building. To be heard, you must file written objections in advance, as provided by law.

Local attorneys were contacted and the Christian Law Association, based in Cleveland, Ohio, was called. They agreed to review the case. On March 22, 1979, a hearing was set at the Muskegon County Circuit Court to hear the church's objection to the tax sale scheduled for May 1. The attorneys for the state did not appear. Mr. Charles Craze, from C.L.A., made a presentation of the case, and the court awarded a default judgment to the church.

The issue was far from over, for on April 23 another hearing was scheduled. Discussion in chambers, not on the record, allowed me an opportunity to explain again that the church was happy to pay any assessment as long as it recognized all churches equally and treated all ministries the same.

That plea was rejected, and we appeared in court again on June 9. The attorney for the township called for the court to set aside the default judgment, explaining that the state had not informed itself of the hearing. Mr. Dick Annis, the local counsel, represented the church well, but the court set the default judgment aside. A lengthy discussion in chambers left a large crowd in the courtroom waiting the outcome. An impasse having been reached, the judge ordered a trial in the case set for August 7 and 8, 1979.

Little time remained for preparation, but it began to sink in that the church property was going to be sold unless God intervened. One more sincere effort was made to broaden the understanding of the township counsel. We requested a hearing at their regular meeting on July 24. It was arranged. Our people attended the meeting and the building was full inside and out. Pastors Nuttall and Rohm presented the case again, and Don Swagman, one of our laymen, gave his testimony. The issue, we repeated, was very simple, "Can the state tell a church what is and is not a ministry of the church?"

The board saw it only as a monetary issue and sat mute. I reflected on our church's ministry in the community since 1941, and asked them if they really intended to sell our property and close our church. We requested they withdraw, but they took no action.

We had taken great care not to share the problem with the news media because we hoped it could be settled. There was, however, a reporter in that meeting. By the next evening the radio, television and newspapers had picked up the story. In the main, the local press was fair to us. It was an issue of religious liberty, an issue of separation of church and state; it was a constitutional question. The state, we said, cannot pick out one ministry and treat it as if it is not a legitimate and integral ministry of Bethel Baptist Church of Fruitport.

The Pretrial Rally

A Freedom Rally was set for the Friday night before the trial. The story of that rally is recorded in the October 1979 issue of the *CLA Defender*. Over a thousand people came, including sixty to eighty preachers. Several came over 250 miles. Levi Whisner, the pioneer of Ohio, Dr. David Gibbs, one of the finest orators, and firey Dr. Earl Little spoke and sent the devil scattering. This was the kind of support it would take. We faced losing the church properties, but I was encouraged.

Into this very unusual scene another interesting circumstance emerged. In God's grace, He took my father Home Sunday morning. The funeral was set for the second day of the trial. Monday was spent in pretrial preparation. Legal documents and papers were gathered from everywhere. The evening was spent at the funeral home with my mother and family.

Tuesday morning, August 7, was a whirlwind: make sure the

radio broadcast was ready; meet Pastor Amstutz and Pastor Rohm; pick up the attorneys at the motel.

Our Day in Court

There we sat. The courtroom was filled. So were the hallways. It couldn't happen here, but it did. If we lost, we would appeal; and if we lost in the end, would we allow Christ's possession to be ripped away? No physical violence, of course, but I would not move. They said they would carry me away to jail. . . .

The judge entered; we were in court. A brief exchange between judge and spectators set the court on edge, but they won his heart before the trial was over. How could one help but like a room full of preachers and a crowd that drove three hours in a bus to support our church? The story that followed is recorded in the September 1979 issue of the *CLA Defender* written in a humorous style by Dan Whisner.

The opening statement by Attorney Craze made our position clear. Separation of church and state was the issue. The school and the church were one. The attorney for the local government protested that direction in his opening statement, but he was overruled.

Pastor Rohm was first on the stand. My heart was pounding. I was happy he was first. For several hours questions as to the validity of the school ministry were calmly handled. The ministries were one; the Bible was the only textbook; all subjects were sacred; yes, math also. After lunch it continued. Finally, Pastor Rohm stepped down. The point had been squarely made.

Next to the stand was Miss Cheryl DeZwaan, staff member teaching kindergarten. Calm, quiet and clear, her testimony was perfect. And now the state's attorney, "No questions, your honor. . . ."

Then it was my turn. My heart was not racing. I could hardly wait for Mr. Craze to get into the meat of the issue. It was a joy to express deep convictions in court, knowing what all of this might cost us. Christian education is a necessity, not a luxury. God commands us to educate in the church. We have no other choice; we must obey God. Are we lawless? No, we obey a higher law. This court gets its authority from the same source. Of course, I am familiar with Romans 13. Would you like an explanation? You wouldn't? The attorney turned to his table. Did we ever have another address for the school? Yes. Shettler Road? No. Was the school ever called Grace Evangelical? No. That's it; he has the record of the improper building. Mr. Craze, that's it!

The township attorney fumbled for an exhibit on the table. Mr. Craze went over to help him find it. Oh, yes, here it is. Your Honor, could we recess until tomorrow; it is almost five. Court adjourned until tomorrow at 9:00 A.M.

The Lord knew what to do and when. We floated out of that courtroom. What a powerful afternoon. Home to clean up, then on to the funeral home. Tomorrow is Dad's funeral.

When we picked up the attorneys the next morning, they loaded their luggage. I wondered what would happen if the trial went a third day. A great crowd was already at the courthouse. Everyone began to settle down, but the attorneys disappeared. We had been through this before and I was concerned. About 9:30 A.M. everyone came bustling in and the judge took his place. Mr. Craze leaned over and said, "They quit." The township attorney was explaining; they had found a clerical error. The billing was improper, illegal and had been originally made to Grace Evangelical School . . . exactly what we had been telling them since 1975. Case dismissed!

There was laughter, tears, hugging and a lot of thanksgiving; attorneys to the airport . . . back to church to face the television cameras . . . to my family . . . and in a few minutes my dad's funeral.

Years of conflict, thousands of dollars. Why? For the conviction of separation of church and state. For religious freedom for the church to choose its own ministry under the will of God without any interference from the state. Congress shall make *no* law prohibiting the free exercise thereof. None, *no, not one,* shouts the blood of dissidents and the saints of God.

To My Critics

Now to those who would take issue with me, to those who would not tell me in the hour of my trial that you thought I was wrong; I love you because there is room for disagreement, but not disagreeableness. This work is not a plea for the state. It is a plea for God's people and the church. ". . . Will ye plead for Baal? . . ." (Judg. 6:31, 32). Then do it carefully. I love this country. I am patriotic after the style of Jeremiah. My praise will be for the righteous who rule well. But I will thunder like a prophet of old about the wickedness I see.

Stand with me now, dear brother. This is a warning of coming conflict. Stand with me now! All hell is set to destroy the church. They have already come for me once and are coming again.

Even if you compromise, someday they will come for you.

In Germany they came first for the Communists, and I didn't speak up because I wasn't a Communist. Then they came for the Jews, and I didn't speak up because I wasn't a Jew. Then they came for the trade unionists, and I didn't speak up because I wasn't a trade unionist. Then they came for the Catholics, and I didn't speak up because I was a Protestant. Then they came for me, and by that time no one was left to speak up.[1]

Footnote

1. Cotham, p. 76.

SELECTED BIBLIOGRAPHY

Books

Barclay, William. *Educational Ideals in the Ancient World.* Grand Rapids: Baker Book House, 1959.

Blamires, Harry. *The Christian Mind.* Ann Arbor: Servant Books, 1963.

Boys, Donald G. *Liberalism: A Rope of Sand.* Indianapolis: Good Hope Press, 1979.

Buswell, James Oliver, Jr. *A Systematic Theology of the Christian Religion.* Vol. I, *Theism and Biblical Anthropology.* Grand Rapids: Zondervan Publishing House, 1962.

Carlyle, A. J. *The Christian Church and Liberty.* New York: George H. Doran Co., 1924.

Conder, Eustace Rogers. "The Relation of the Church to the State," in *Ecclesia: Church Problems Considered,* Henry Robert Reynolds, ed. London: Hodder & Stoughton, 1870.

Cotham, Perry C. *Politics, Americanism and Christianity.* Grand Rapids: Baker Book House, 1976.

Culver, Robert Duncan, *Toward a Biblical View of Civil Government.* Chicago: Moody Press, 1975.

Cuninggim, Merrimon. *Freedom's Holy Light.* New York: Harper & Brothers, 1955.

Dale, A. W. W. *The Life of R. W. Dale of Birmingham.* London: Hodder & Stoughton, 1898.

Dale, R. W. *Fellowship with Christ.* London: Hodder & Stoughton, 1907.

de Chalandeau, Alexander. *The Christians in the U.S.S.R.* Chicago: Harper and Co., 1978.

Dowley, Tim, ed. *Eerdman's Handbook to the History of Christianity.* Grand Rapids: Wm. B. Eerdmans Publishing Co., 1977.

Foxe, John. *Foxe's Christian Martyrs of the World.* Chicago: Moody Press, n.d.

Fuller, David Otis, ed. *Valiant for the Truth.* New York: McGraw-Hill Book Co., 1961.

Garrett, John. *Roger Williams: Witness Beyond Christendom—1603-1683.* London: Collier-Macmillan Ltd., 1970.

Griffith, Gwilym O. *John Bunyan.* London: Hodder & Stoughton, 1927.

Grover, Alan N. *Ohio's Trojan Horse.* Greenville, SC: Bob Jones University Press, 1977.

Hall, Verna, comp., Joseph Allan Montgomery, ed. *Self-Government with Union: Christian History of the Constitution Series,* Vol. II. San Francisco: The American Christian Constitution Press, 1962.

Hiscox, Edward T. *The New Directory for Baptist Churches.* Valley Forge, PA: Judson Press, 1894; reprint ed., Grand Rapids: Kregel Publications, 1970.

Hough, Lynn Harold. *Whither Christianity?* New York: Harper & Brothers, 1929.

Huegli, Albert G., ed. *Church and State under God.* St. Louis: Concordia Publishing House, 1964.

Kelley, Dean M. *Why Churches Should Not Pay Taxes.* New York: Harper & Row, 1977.

Kik, J. Marcellus. *Church and State.* New York: Thomas Nelson & Sons, 1963.

Langford, Norman F. *Fire Upon the Earth.* Philadelphia: The Westminster Press, 1940.

Latourette, Kenneth Scott. *A History of Christianity.* New York: Harper & Brothers, 1953.

Lee, Umphrey. *Render unto the People.* New York: Abingdon-Cokesbury Press, 1947.

Loetscher, Lefferts A., ed. *Twentieth Century Encyclopedia of Religous Knowledge,* Vol. I. Grand Rapids: Baker Book House, 1955.

Luther, Martin. *Epistle to the Galatians.* Philadelphia: Salmon S. Miles, 1840.

Marshall, Peter and David Manuel. *The Light and the Glory.* Old Tappan, NJ: Fleming H. Revell Co., 1977.

Mecklin, John M. *The Story of American Dissent.* New York: Harcourt, Brace and Co., 1934.

Morris, Henry M. *Education for the Real World.* San Diego: Creation-Life Publishers, 1977.

Mouw, Richard J. *Politics and the Biblical Drama.* Grand Rapids: Wm. B. Eerdmans Publishing Co., 1976.

Moyer, Elgin. *Great Leaders of the Christian Church.* Chicago: Moody Press, 1951.

Newman, Albert Henry. *A Manual of Church History,* Vol. II. Valley Forge, PA: Judson Press, 1902.

Newman, Robert C. *Baptists and the American Tradition.* Schaumburg, IL: Regular Baptist Press, 1976.

Nygaard, Norman E. *Champion of Liberty.* Grand Rapids: Zondervan Publishing House, 1964.

Peterson, Walfred H. *Thy Liberty in Law.* Nashville: Convention Press, 1978.

Pickering, Ernest. *Biblical Separation: The Struggle for a Pure Church.* Schaumburg, IL: Regular Baptist Press, 1979.

Rowe, Henry Kalloch. *The History of Religon of the United States.* New York: The Macmillan Co., 1928.

Ryrie, Charles Caldwell. *Biblical Theology of the New Testament.* Chicago: Moody Press, 1959.

Schaeffer, Francis A. *How Should We Then Live?* Old Tappan, NJ: Fleming H. Revell Co., 1976.

Seebohm, Frederic. "The Era of the Protestant Revolution." Edward E. Morris, ed. Series on the *Epochs of History,* No. 1. New York: Scribner Armstrong, and Co., 1874.

Slater, Rosalie J. *Teaching and Learning America's Christian History.* San Francisco: Foundation for American Christian Education, 1973.

Vedder, Henry C. *A Short History of the Baptists.* Valley Forge, PA: Judson Press, 1907.

Whitehead, John W. *The Separation Illusion.* Milford, MI: Mott Media, 1977.

Scripture Citations

The Holy Bible. All Scripture citations (except where otherwise noted) are from the Authorized Version of 1611.

Periodicals, Newsletters, Newspapers

Banas, Teri. "Warrant Asked for Minister by Prosecutor," *Plymouth Observer* (October 22, 1979).

"Bd. of Ed. vs. James Olin," *CLA Defender* (November 1978).

Biscoe, B. Robert, ed. *Fundamental News Service.* Valley Forge, PA: American Council of Christian Churches, n.d.

"Briefcase: Wisconsin," *CLA Defender* (October 1979).

"City of Concord vs. New Testament Baptist Church—Heritage Christian School," *CLA Defender* (March 1978).

Cooley, John. "Victory in Frankfort," *CLA Defender* (November 1978).

"Federal Grip on Schools Tightens." *The National Laymen's Digest* (November 1979).

Frodge, Dan and Kye Harris. "Why We Went to Jail," *CLA Defender* (August 1979).
"From the Editor's Desk." *The Communicator* (September-October 1979).
Hallberg, Dean. "Jonestown—Background and Backlash," *Faith for the Family* (November 1979).
Hardaway, Gary. "Will the Government Raise Your Child?" *Moody Monthly* (November 1979).
"Indiana Impact." *CLA Defender* (March 1978).
"Is Baptist Temple Safe?" *The Solon Times* (September 21, 1978).
Little, Earl. "The CLA Briefcase." *CLA Defender* (March 1979).
"Louisiana Wins on Tax Credit Plan." *Freedom in Education* (July-August, September 1979).
McNulty, Timothy. "Church and State in a Life-and-Death Education Battle." *Detroit Free Press* (May 2, 1979).
"Nebraska Update." *CLA Defender* (August 1979).
Rushdoony, R. J. "Is Separation of Church and State Really Religious Freedom?" *Cornerstone* (June 1979).
Sanchez, Diane. "Freedom Rally." *The Flaming Torch* (January 1979).
"Settle Temple Differences." *The Solon Times* (September 21, 1978).
"State of Tennessee Preparing Case Against U.S. Labor Department." *CLA Defender* (October 1979).
"Tampa Suit Settled." *CLA Defender* (October 1979).
"Tax Foreclosure Against California Baptist Congregation." *CLA Defender* (October 1979).
"Terror in the Schools." *U.S. News & World Report* (January 26, 1976).
Thompson, Roy. "It's Still Licensure." *CLA Defender* (June 1978).
"Update: Benton, Arkansas, Westside Baptist Church Victory." *CLA Defender* (January 1979).
"Update: Marshall, Texas." *CLA Defender* (January 1979).
"Vacation Bible School Ruled Illegal in Canada." *CLA Defender* (September 1979).
"Victory Rings in Tujunga, California." *CLA Defender* (December 1978).
"Warrant Asked for Minister by Prosecutor." *Plymouth Observer* (October 22, 1979).
Whisner, Dan. "That Is the Question." *CLA Defender* (August 1979).

Addresses

Address delivered July 4, 1821, from the rostrum of the House of Representatives on the occasion of reading the Declaration of Independence.

Bicentennial speech at Plymouth, Massachusetts, celebrating the landing of the Pilgrims, 1820.
Farewell address in Springfield, Illinois, on February 11, 1861, before taking office of President of the United States.
"Precepts of Our Pilgrim Heritage." Address of Lt. General James V. Edmundson, U.S. Air Force (Ret.) to the Florida State Meeting of the Order of Founders and Patriots, January 20, 1979, in*News & Views* (November 1979).
Report of the Committee of Correspondence to the Boston Town Meeting, November 20, 1772.

Legal Sources

Engel v. Vitale, 370 U.S. 421 (1962).
State v. Whisner, 47 Ohio St. 181 at 213, 214 (1976).

Pamphlets

Villers, T. J. *Fidelity to Our Baptist Heritage,* ed. by R. T. Ketcham. Schaumburg, IL: General Association of Regular Baptist Churches, n.d.
Williamson, Jerry. *Is Your Child a Ward of the State Church?* Fort Lauderdale: Gold Coast Christian School, n.d.